Munro Bagging Log Book

Belongs to:

_____

Contents

Beinn Teallach
915m

Date: _____ Weather: _____ Temperature: _____

Start time: _____ End time: _____ Total distance: _____

Climb rating: ☆ ☆ ☆ ☆ ☆   Difficulty: 1 2 3 4 5

Companions: _____

_____

_____

Favourite moment: _____

_____

_____

Notes: _____

_____

_____

_____

_____

_____

_____

_____

_____

Carn Aosda
915m

Date: _____ Weather: _____ Temperature: _____

Start time: _____ End time: _____ Total distance: _____

Climb rating: ☆ ☆ ☆ ☆ ☆　Difficulty:　1　2　3　4　5

Companions: _____

_____

_____

Favourite moment: _____

_____

_____

Notes: _____

_____

_____

_____

_____

_____

_____

_____

_____

_____

Ben Vane
916m

Date: _____ Weather: _____ Temperature: _____

Start time: _____ End time: _____ Total distance: _____

Climb rating: ☆ ☆ ☆ ☆ ☆   Difficulty: 1 2 3 4 5

Companions: _____

_____

_____

Favourite moment: _____

_____

_____

Notes: _____

_____

_____

_____

_____

_____

_____

_____

_____

_____

Beinn a' Chleibh
916m

Date: _____ Weather: _____ Temperature: _____

Start time: _____ End time: _____ Total distance: _____

Climb rating: ☆ ☆ ☆ ☆ ☆   Difficulty: 1 2 3 4 5

Companions: _____

_____

_____

Favourite moment: _____

_____

_____

Notes: _____

_____

_____

_____

_____

_____

_____

_____

_____

_____

_____

Meall na Teanga
917m

Date: _____ Weather: _____ Temperature: _____

Start time: _____ End time: _____ Total distance: _____

Climb rating: ☆ ☆ ☆ ☆ ☆   Difficulty: 1 2 3 4 5

Companions: _____

_____

_____

Favourite moment: _____

_____

_____

Notes: _____

_____

_____

_____

_____

_____

_____

_____

_____

_____

_____

Geal-charn (Drumochter)
917m

Date: _____ Weather: _____ Temperature: _____

Start time: _____ End time: _____ Total distance: _____

Climb rating: ☆ ☆ ☆ ☆ ☆   Difficulty: 1 2 3 4 5

Companions: _____

_____

_____

Favourite moment: _____

_____

_____

Notes: _____

_____

_____

_____

_____

_____

_____

_____

_____

Creag nan Damh
917m

Date: _____ Weather: _____ Temperature: _____

Start time: _____ End time: _____ Total distance: _____

Climb rating: ☆ ☆ ☆ ☆ ☆   Difficulty: 1 2 3 4 5

Companions: _____

_____

_____

Favourite moment: _____

_____

_____

Notes: _____

_____

_____

_____

_____

_____

_____

_____

_____

Sgurr a' Mhadaidh
918m

Date: _____ Weather: _____ Temperature: _____

Start time: _____ End time: _____ Total distance: _____

Climb rating: ☆ ☆ ☆ ☆ ☆   Difficulty: 1 2 3 4 5

Companions: _____

_____

_____

Favourite moment: _____

_____

_____

Notes: _____

_____

_____

_____

_____

_____

_____

_____

_____

_____

_____

A Ghlas-bheinn
918m

Date: _____ Weather: _____ Temperature: _____

Start time: _____ End time: _____ Total distance: _____

Climb rating: ☆ ☆ ☆ ☆ ☆   Difficulty: 1 2 3 4 5

Companions: _____

_____

_____

Favourite moment: _____

_____

_____

Notes: _____

_____

_____

_____

_____

_____

_____

_____

_____

_____

Ruadh Stac Mor
919m

Date: _____ Weather: _____ Temperature: _____

Start time: _____ End time: _____ Total distance: _____

Climb rating: ☆ ☆ ☆ ☆ ☆   Difficulty: 1 2 3 4 5

Companions: _____

_____

_____

Favourite moment: _____

_____

_____

Notes: _____

_____

_____

_____

_____

_____

_____

_____

_____

_____

_____

Gairich
919m

Date: _____ Weather: _____ Temperature: _____

Start time: _____ End time: _____ Total distance: _____

Climb rating: ☆ ☆ ☆ ☆ ☆   Difficulty: 1 2 3 4 5

Companions: _____

_____

_____

Favourite moment: _____

_____

_____

Notes: _____

_____

_____

_____

_____

_____

_____

_____

_____

_____

Sgiath Chuil
920m

Date: _____ Weather: _____ Temperature: _____

Start time: _____ End time: _____ Total distance: _____

Climb rating: ☆ ☆ ☆ ☆ ☆   Difficulty: 1 2 3 4 5

Companions: _____

_____

_____

Favourite moment: _____

_____

_____

Notes: _____

_____

_____

_____

_____

_____

_____

_____

_____

_____

Carn Sgulain
920m

Date: _____ Weather: _____ Temperature: _____

Start time: _____ End time: _____ Total distance: _____

Climb rating: ☆ ☆ ☆ ☆ ☆   Difficulty: 1 2 3 4 5

Companions: _____

_____

_____

Favourite moment: _____

_____

_____

Notes: _____

_____

_____

_____

_____

_____

_____

_____

_____

_____

_____

An Socach (Affric)
921m

Date: _____ Weather: _____ Temperature: _____

Start time: _____ End time: _____ Total distance: _____

Climb rating: ☆ ☆ ☆ ☆ ☆   Difficulty: 1 2 3 4 5

Companions: _____

_____

_____

Favourite moment: _____

_____

_____

Notes: _____

_____

_____

_____

_____

_____

_____

_____

_____

Beinn Alligin - Tom na Gruagaich
922m

Date: _____ Weather: _____ Temperature: _____

Start time: _____ End time: _____ Total distance: _____

Climb rating: ☆ ☆ ☆ ☆ ☆   Difficulty: 1 2 3 4 5

Companions: _____

_____

_____

Favourite moment: _____

_____

_____

Notes: _____

_____

_____

_____

_____

_____

_____

_____

_____

Sgurr nan Each
923m

Date: _____ Weather: _____ Temperature: _____

Start time: _____ End time: _____ Total distance: _____

Climb rating: ☆ ☆ ☆ ☆ ☆   Difficulty: 1 2 3 4 5

Companions: _____

_____

_____

Favourite moment: _____

_____

_____

Notes: _____

_____

_____

_____

_____

_____

_____

_____

_____

_____

An Coileachan
924m

Date: _____ Weather: _____ Temperature: _____

Start time: _____ End time: _____ Total distance: _____

Climb rating: ☆ ☆ ☆ ☆ ☆   Difficulty: 1 2 3 4 5

Companions: _____

_____

_____

Favourite moment: _____

_____

_____

Notes: _____

_____

_____

_____

_____

_____

_____

_____

_____

_____

Creag Pitridh
924m

Date: _____ Weather: _____ Temperature: _____

Start time: _____ End time: _____ Total distance: _____

Climb rating: ☆ ☆ ☆ ☆ ☆ Difficulty: 1 2 3 4 5

Companions: _____

_____

_____

Favourite moment: _____

_____

_____

Notes: _____

_____

_____

_____

_____

_____

_____

_____

_____

Etive Beag - Stob Coire Raineach
925m

Date: _____ Weather: _____ Temperature: _____

Start time: _____ End time: _____ Total distance: _____

Climb rating: ☆ ☆ ☆ ☆ ☆   Difficulty: 1 2 3 4 5

Companions: _____

_____

_____

Favourite moment: _____

_____

_____

Notes: _____

_____

_____

_____

_____

_____

_____

_____

_____

Meall a' Choire Leith
926m

Date: _____   Weather: _____   Temperature: _____

Start time: _____   End time: _____   Total distance: _____

Climb rating: ☆ ☆ ☆ ☆ ☆   Difficulty: 1 2 3 4 5

Companions: _____

_____

_____

Favourite moment: _____

_____

_____

Notes: _____

_____

_____

_____

_____

_____

_____

_____

_____

_____

_____

Seana Bhraig
926m

Date: _____ Weather: _____ Temperature: _____

Start time: _____ End time: _____ Total distance: _____

Climb rating: ☆ ☆ ☆ ☆ ☆   Difficulty: 1 2 3 4 5

Companions: _____

_____

_____

Favourite moment: _____

_____

_____

Notes: _____

_____

_____

_____

_____

_____

_____

_____

_____

_____

Beinn Liath Mhor
926m

Date: _____ Weather: _____ Temperature: _____

Start time: _____ End time: _____ Total distance: _____

Climb rating: ☆ ☆ ☆ ☆ ☆ Difficulty: 1 2 3 4 5

Companions: _____

_____

_____

Favourite moment: _____

_____

_____

Notes: _____

_____

_____

_____

_____

_____

_____

_____

_____

_____

Geal Charn (Monadhliath)
926m

Date: _____ Weather: _____ Temperature: _____

Start time: _____ End time: _____ Total distance: _____

Climb rating: ☆ ☆ ☆ ☆ ☆   Difficulty: 1 2 3 4 5

Companions: _____

_____

_____

Favourite moment: _____

_____

_____

Notes: _____

_____

_____

_____

_____

_____

_____

_____

_____

_____

Sgurr nan Eag
926m

Date: _____ Weather: _____ Temperature: _____

Start time: _____ End time: _____ Total distance: _____

Climb rating: ☆ ☆ ☆ ☆ ☆   Difficulty: 1 2 3 4 5

Companions: _____

_____

_____

Favourite moment: _____

_____

_____

Notes: _____

_____

_____

_____

_____

_____

_____

_____

_____

_____

Ben Hope
927m

Date: _____ Weather: _____ Temperature: _____

Start time: _____ End time: _____ Total distance: _____

Climb rating: ☆ ☆ ☆ ☆ ☆   Difficulty: 1 2 3 4 5

Companions: _____

_____

_____

Favourite moment: _____

_____

_____

Notes: _____

_____

_____

_____

_____

_____

_____

_____

_____

Eididh nan Clach Geala
927m

Date: _____ Weather: _____ Temperature: _____

Start time: _____ End time: _____ Total distance: _____

Climb rating: ☆ ☆ ☆ ☆ ☆   Difficulty: 1 2 3 4 5

Companions: _____

_____

_____

Favourite moment: _____

_____

_____

Notes: _____

_____

_____

_____

_____

_____

_____

_____

_____

_____

Beinn Narnain
927m

Date: _____ Weather: _____ Temperature: _____

Start time: _____ End time: _____ Total distance: _____

Climb rating: ☆ ☆ ☆ ☆ ☆   Difficulty: 1 2 3 4 5

Companions: _____

_____

_____

Favourite moment: _____

_____

_____

Notes: _____

_____

_____

_____

_____

_____

_____

_____

_____

Moruisg
928m

Date: _____ Weather: _____ Temperature: _____

Start time: _____ End time: _____ Total distance: _____

Climb rating: ☆ ☆ ☆ ☆ ☆   Difficulty: 1 2 3 4 5

Companions: _____

_____

_____

Favourite moment: _____

_____

_____

Notes: _____

_____

_____

_____

_____

_____

_____

_____

_____

_____

_____

Mayar
928m

Date: _____ Weather: _____ Temperature: _____

Start time: _____ End time: _____ Total distance: _____

Climb rating: ☆ ☆ ☆ ☆ ☆   Difficulty: 1 2 3 4 5

Companions: _____

_____

_____

Favourite moment: _____

_____

_____

Notes: _____

_____

_____

_____

_____

_____

_____

_____

_____

_____

Meall nan Eun
928m

Date: _____ Weather: _____ Temperature: _____

Start time: _____ End time: _____ Total distance: _____

Climb rating: ☆ ☆ ☆ ☆ ☆   Difficulty: 1 2 3 4 5

Companions: _____

_____

_____

Favourite moment: _____

_____

_____

Notes: _____

_____

_____

_____

_____

_____

_____

_____

_____

_____

Blaven (Bla Bheinn)
929m

Date: _____ Weather: _____ Temperature: _____

Start time: _____ End time: _____ Total distance: _____

Climb rating: ☆ ☆ ☆ ☆ ☆   Difficulty: 1 2 3 4 5

Companions: _____

_____

_____

Favourite moment: _____

_____

_____

Notes: _____

_____

_____

_____

_____

_____

_____

_____

_____

A' Chailleach (Monadhliath)
929m

Date: _____ Weather: _____ Temperature: _____

Start time: _____ End time: _____ Total distance: _____

Climb rating: ☆ ☆ ☆ ☆ ☆   Difficulty: 1 2 3 4 5

Companions: _____

_____

_____

Favourite moment: _____

_____

_____

Notes: _____

_____

_____

_____

_____

_____

_____

_____

_____

_____

Beinn Bhreac
931m

Date: _____ Weather: _____ Temperature: _____

Start time: _____ End time: _____ Total distance: _____

Climb rating: ☆ ☆ ☆ ☆ ☆   Difficulty: 1 2 3 4 5

Companions: _____

_____

_____

Favourite moment: _____

_____

_____

Notes: _____

_____

_____

_____

_____

_____

_____

_____

_____

_____

Ben Chonzie
931m

Date: _____ Weather: _____ Temperature: _____

Start time: _____ End time: _____ Total distance: _____

Climb rating: ☆ ☆ ☆ ☆ ☆   Difficulty: 1 2 3 4 5

Companions: _____

_____

_____

Favourite moment: _____

_____

_____

Notes: _____

_____

_____

_____

_____

_____

_____

_____

_____

_____

Meall Buidhe (Lyon)
932m

Date: _____ Weather: _____ Temperature: _____

Start time: _____ End time: _____ Total distance: _____

Climb rating: ☆ ☆ ☆ ☆ ☆   Difficulty: 1 2 3 4 5

Companions: _____

_____

_____

Favourite moment: _____

_____

_____

Notes: _____

_____

_____

_____

_____

_____

_____

_____

_____

Beinn Chabhair
932m

Date: _____ Weather: _____ Temperature: _____

Start time: _____ End time: _____ Total distance: _____

Climb rating: ☆ ☆ ☆ ☆ ☆   Difficulty: 1 2 3 4 5

Companions: _____

_____

_____

Favourite moment: _____

_____

_____

Notes: _____

_____

_____

_____

_____

_____

_____

_____

_____

_____

Fionn Bheinn
933m

Date: _____ Weather: _____ Temperature: _____

Start time: _____ End time: _____ Total distance: _____

Climb rating: ☆ ☆ ☆ ☆ ☆   Difficulty: 1 2 3 4 5

Companions: _____

_____

_____

Favourite moment: _____

_____

_____

Notes: _____

_____

_____

_____

_____

_____

_____

_____

_____

_____

Maol Chean-dearg
933m

Date: _____ Weather: _____ Temperature: _____

Start time: _____ End time: _____ Total distance: _____

Climb rating: ☆ ☆ ☆ ☆ ☆   Difficulty: 1 2 3 4 5

Companions: _____

_____

_____

Favourite moment: _____

_____

_____

Notes: _____

_____

_____

_____

_____

_____

_____

_____

_____

_____

The Cairnwell
933m

Date: _____ Weather: _____ Temperature: _____

Start time: _____ End time: _____ Total distance: _____

Climb rating: ☆ ☆ ☆ ☆ ☆   Difficulty: 1 2 3 4 5

Companions: _____

_____

_____

Favourite moment: _____

_____

_____

Notes: _____

_____

_____

_____

_____

_____

_____

_____

_____

_____

Beinn Tarsuinn
934m

Date: _____ Weather: _____ Temperature: _____

Start time: _____ End time: _____ Total distance: _____

Climb rating: ☆ ☆ ☆ ☆ ☆   Difficulty: 1 2 3 4 5

Companions: _____

_____

_____

Favourite moment: _____

_____

_____

Notes: _____

_____

_____

_____

_____

_____

_____

_____

_____

_____

Am Basteir
934m

Date: _____   Weather: _____   Temperature: _____

Start time: _____   End time: _____   Total distance: _____

Climb rating: ☆ ☆ ☆ ☆ ☆   Difficulty: 1 2 3 4 5

Companions: _____

_____

_____

Favourite moment: _____

_____

_____

Notes: _____

_____

_____

_____

_____

_____

_____

_____

_____

Meall a' Chrasgaidh
934m

Date: _____ Weather: _____ Temperature: _____

Start time: _____ End time: _____ Total distance: _____

Climb rating: ☆ ☆ ☆ ☆ ☆   Difficulty: 1 2 3 4 5

Companions: _____

_____

_____

Favourite moment: _____

_____

_____

Notes: _____

_____

_____

_____

_____

_____

_____

_____

_____

_____

Beinn na Lap
935m

Date: _____ Weather: _____ Temperature: _____

Start time: _____ End time: _____ Total distance: _____

Climb rating: ☆ ☆ ☆ ☆ ☆   Difficulty: 1 2 3 4 5

Companions: _____

_____

_____

Favourite moment: _____

_____

_____

Notes: _____

_____

_____

_____

_____

_____

_____

_____

_____

A' Bhuidheanach Bheag
936m

Date: _____ Weather: _____ Temperature: _____

Start time: _____ End time: _____ Total distance: _____

Climb rating: ☆ ☆ ☆ ☆ ☆   Difficulty: 1 2 3 4 5

Companions: _____

_____

_____

Favourite moment: _____

_____

_____

Notes: _____

_____

_____

_____

_____

_____

_____

_____

_____

_____

_____

Sron a' Choire Ghairbh
937m

Date: _____ Weather: _____ Temperature: _____

Start time: _____ End time: _____ Total distance: _____

Climb rating: ☆ ☆ ☆ ☆ ☆   Difficulty: 1 2 3 4 5

Companions: _____

_____

_____

Favourite moment: _____

_____

_____

Notes: _____

_____

_____

_____

_____

_____

_____

_____

_____

Beinn Sgulaird
937m

Date: _____ Weather: _____ Temperature: _____

Start time: _____ End time: _____ Total distance: _____

Climb rating: ☆ ☆ ☆ ☆ ☆ Difficulty: 1 2 3 4 5

Companions: _____

_____

_____

Favourite moment: _____

_____

_____

Notes: _____

_____

_____

_____

_____

_____

_____

_____

_____

Luinne Bheinn
939m

Date: _____ Weather: _____ Temperature: _____

Start time: _____ End time: _____ Total distance: _____

Climb rating: ☆ ☆ ☆ ☆ ☆   Difficulty: 1 2 3 4 5

Companions: _____

_____

_____

Favourite moment: _____

_____

_____

Notes: _____

_____

_____

_____

_____

_____

_____

_____

_____

_____

Mount Keen
939m

Date: _____ Weather: _____ Temperature: _____

Start time: _____ End time: _____ Total distance: _____

Climb rating: ☆ ☆ ☆ ☆ ☆   Difficulty: 1 2 3 4 5

Companions: _____

_____

_____

Favourite moment: _____

_____

_____

Notes: _____

_____

_____

_____

_____

_____

_____

_____

_____

_____

Mullach nan Coirean
939m

Date: _____ Weather: _____ Temperature: _____

Start time: _____ End time: _____ Total distance: _____

Climb rating: ☆ ☆ ☆ ☆ ☆   Difficulty: 1 2 3 4 5

Companions: _____

_____

_____

Favourite moment: _____

_____

_____

Notes: _____

_____

_____

_____

_____

_____

_____

_____

_____

_____

Carn na Caim
941m

Date: _____ Weather: _____ Temperature: _____

Start time: _____ End time: _____ Total distance: _____

Climb rating: ☆ ☆ ☆ ☆ ☆   Difficulty: 1 2 3 4 5

Companions: _____

_____

_____

Favourite moment: _____

_____

_____

Notes: _____

_____

_____

_____

_____

_____

_____

_____

_____

Carn Dearg (Ossian)
941m

Date: _____ Weather: _____ Temperature: _____

Start time: _____ End time: _____ Total distance: _____

Climb rating: ☆ ☆ ☆ ☆ ☆   Difficulty: 1 2 3 4 5

Companions: _____

_____

_____

Favourite moment: _____

_____

_____

Notes: _____

_____

_____

_____

_____

_____

_____

_____

_____

Beinn a' Chroin
941m

Date: _____ Weather: _____ Temperature: _____

Start time: _____ End time: _____ Total distance: _____

Climb rating: ☆ ☆ ☆ ☆ ☆   Difficulty: 1 2 3 4 5

Companions: _____

_____

_____

Favourite moment: _____

_____

_____

Notes: _____

_____

_____

_____

_____

_____

_____

_____

_____

_____

Binnein Beag
943m

Date: _____ Weather: _____ Temperature: _____

Start time: _____ End time: _____ Total distance: _____

Climb rating: ☆ ☆ ☆ ☆ ☆   Difficulty: 1 2 3 4 5

Companions: _____

_____

_____

Favourite moment: _____

_____

_____

Notes: _____

_____

_____

_____

_____

_____

_____

_____

_____

_____

Ben Vorlich (Arrochar)
943m

Date: _____ Weather: _____ Temperature: _____

Start time: _____ End time: _____ Total distance: _____

Climb rating: ☆ ☆ ☆ ☆ ☆   Difficulty: 1 2 3 4 5

Companions: _____

_____

_____

Favourite moment: _____

_____

_____

Notes: _____

_____

_____

_____

_____

_____

_____

_____

_____

Sgurr Dubh Mor
944m

Date: _____ Weather: _____ Temperature: _____

Start time: _____ End time: _____ Total distance: _____

Climb rating: ☆ ☆ ☆ ☆ ☆   Difficulty: 1 2 3 4 5

Companions: _____

_____

_____

Favourite moment: _____

_____

_____

Notes: _____

_____

_____

_____

_____

_____

_____

_____

_____

An Socach (Glen Ey)
944m

Date: _____ Weather: _____ Temperature: _____

Start time: _____ End time: _____ Total distance: _____

Climb rating: ☆ ☆ ☆ ☆ ☆   Difficulty: 1 2 3 4 5

Companions: _____

_____

_____

Favourite moment: _____

_____

_____

Notes: _____

_____

_____

_____

_____

_____

_____

_____

_____

_____

Bidein a' Choire Sheasgaich
945m

Date: _____ Weather: _____ Temperature: _____

Start time: _____ End time: _____ Total distance: _____

Climb rating: ☆ ☆ ☆ ☆ ☆   Difficulty: 1 2 3 4 5

Companions: _____

_____

_____

Favourite moment: _____

_____

_____

Notes: _____

_____

_____

_____

_____

_____

_____

_____

_____

_____

Stob a' Choire Odhair
945m

Date: _____ Weather: _____ Temperature: _____

Start time: _____ End time: _____ Total distance: _____

Climb rating: ☆ ☆ ☆ ☆ ☆   Difficulty: 1 2 3 4 5

Companions: _____

_____

_____

Favourite moment: _____

_____

_____

Notes: _____

_____

_____

_____

_____

_____

_____

_____

_____

_____

Carn Bhac
945m

Date: _____   Weather: _____   Temperature: _____

Start time: _____   End time: _____   Total distance: _____

Climb rating: ☆ ☆ ☆ ☆ ☆   Difficulty: 1 2 3 4 5

Companions: _____

_____

_____

Favourite moment: _____

_____

_____

Notes: _____

_____

_____

_____

_____

_____

_____

_____

_____

_____

_____

Carn Dearg
946m

Date: _____ Weather: _____ Temperature: _____

Start time: _____ End time: _____ Total distance: _____

Climb rating: ☆ ☆ ☆ ☆ ☆   Difficulty: 1 2 3 4 5

Companions: _____

_____

_____

Favourite moment: _____

_____

_____

Notes: _____

_____

_____

_____

_____

_____

_____

_____

_____

_____

Beinn Tulaichean
946m

Date: _____ Weather: _____ Temperature: _____

Start time: _____ End time: _____ Total distance: _____

Climb rating: ☆ ☆ ☆ ☆ ☆   Difficulty: 1 2 3 4 5

Companions: _____

_____

_____

Favourite moment: _____

_____

_____

Notes: _____

_____

_____

_____

_____

_____

_____

_____

_____

_____

Meall Buidhe
946m

Date: _____ Weather: _____ Temperature: _____

Start time: _____ End time: _____ Total distance: _____

Climb rating: ☆ ☆ ☆ ☆ ☆   Difficulty: 1 2 3 4 5

Companions: _____

_____

_____

Favourite moment: _____

_____

_____

Notes: _____

_____

_____

_____

_____

_____

_____

_____

_____

Sgurr na Sgine
946m

Date: _____ Weather: _____ Temperature: _____

Start time: _____ End time: _____ Total distance: _____

Climb rating: ☆ ☆ ☆ ☆ ☆   Difficulty: 1 2 3 4 5

Companions: _____

_____

_____

Favourite moment: _____

_____

_____

Notes: _____

_____

_____

_____

_____

_____

_____

_____

_____

Creag a' Mhaim
946m

Date: _____ Weather: _____ Temperature: _____

Start time: _____ End time: _____ Total distance: _____

Climb rating: ☆ ☆ ☆ ☆ ☆   Difficulty: 1 2 3 4 5

Companions: _____

_____

_____

Favourite moment: _____

_____

_____

Notes: _____

_____

_____

_____

_____

_____

_____

_____

_____

Driesh
947m

Date: _____ Weather: _____ Temperature: _____

Start time: _____ End time: _____ Total distance: _____

Climb rating: ☆ ☆ ☆ ☆ ☆   Difficulty: 1 2 3 4 5

Companions: _____

_____

_____

Favourite moment: _____

_____

_____

Notes: _____

_____

_____

_____

_____

_____

_____

_____

_____

Sgurr Mhic Choinnich
948m

Date: _____ Weather: _____ Temperature: _____

Start time: _____ End time: _____ Total distance: _____

Climb rating: ☆ ☆ ☆ ☆ ☆   Difficulty: 1 2 3 4 5

Companions: _____

_____

_____

Favourite moment: _____

_____

_____

Notes: _____

_____

_____

_____

_____

_____

_____

_____

_____

Beinn Buidhe (Knoydart)
949m

Date: _____ Weather: _____ Temperature: _____

Start time: _____ End time: _____ Total distance: _____

Climb rating: ☆ ☆ ☆ ☆ ☆   Difficulty: 1 2 3 4 5

Companions: _____

_____

_____

Favourite moment: _____

_____

_____

Notes: _____

_____

_____

_____

_____

_____

_____

_____

_____

_____

_____

Meall Gorm
949m

Date: _____ Weather: _____ Temperature: _____

Start time: _____ End time: _____ Total distance: _____

Climb rating: ☆ ☆ ☆ ☆ ☆   Difficulty: 1 2 3 4 5

Companions: _____

_____

_____

Favourite moment: _____

_____

_____

Notes: _____

_____

_____

_____

_____

_____

_____

_____

_____

_____

Meall Chuaich
951m

Date: _____ Weather: _____ Temperature: _____

Start time: _____ End time: _____ Total distance: _____

Climb rating: ☆ ☆ ☆ ☆ ☆   Difficulty: 1 2 3 4 5

Companions: _____

_____

_____

Favourite moment: _____

_____

_____

Notes: _____

_____

_____

_____

_____

_____

_____

_____

_____

Aonach Eacgach - Meall Dearg
952m

Date: _____ Weather: _____ Temperature: _____

Start time: _____ End time: _____ Total distance: _____

Climb rating: ☆ ☆ ☆ ☆ ☆   Difficulty: 1 2 3 4 5

Companions: _____

_____

_____

Favourite moment: _____

_____

_____

Notes: _____

_____

_____

_____

_____

_____

_____

_____

_____

_____

Am Faochagach
953m

Date: _____ Weather: _____ Temperature: _____

Start time: _____ End time: _____ Total distance: _____

Climb rating: ☆ ☆ ☆ ☆ ☆   Difficulty: 1 2 3 4 5

Companions: _____

_____

_____

Favourite moment: _____

_____

_____

Notes: _____

_____

_____

_____

_____

_____

_____

_____

_____

Beinn Mhanach
953m

Date: _____ Weather: _____ Temperature: _____

Start time: _____ End time: _____ Total distance: _____

Climb rating: ☆ ☆ ☆ ☆ ☆   Difficulty: 1 2 3 4 5

Companions: _____

_____

_____

Favourite moment: _____

_____

_____

Notes: _____

_____

_____

_____

_____

_____

_____

_____

_____

_____

Stob na Broige
953m

Date: _____ Weather: _____ Temperature: _____

Start time: _____ End time: _____ Total distance: _____

Climb rating: ☆ ☆ ☆ ☆ ☆   Difficulty: 1 2 3 4 5

Companions: _____

_____

_____

Favourite moment: _____

_____

_____

Notes: _____

_____

_____

_____

_____

_____

_____

_____

_____

Sgurr nan Coireachan (Dessary)
954m

Date: _____ Weather: _____ Temperature: _____

Start time: _____ End time: _____ Total distance: _____

Climb rating: ☆ ☆ ☆ ☆ ☆   Difficulty: 1 2 3 4 5

Companions: _____

_____

_____

Favourite moment: _____

_____

_____

Notes: _____

_____

_____

_____

_____

_____

_____

_____

_____

_____

Beinn Liath Mhor Fannaich
954m

Date: _____ Weather: _____ Temperature: _____

Start time: _____ End time: _____ Total distance: _____

Climb rating: ☆ ☆ ☆ ☆ ☆   Difficulty: 1 2 3 4 5

Companions: _____

_____

_____

Favourite moment: _____

_____

_____

Notes: _____

_____

_____

_____

_____

_____

_____

_____

_____

Sgor Gaibhre
955m

Date: _____ Weather: _____ Temperature: _____

Start time: _____ End time: _____ Total distance: _____

Climb rating: ☆ ☆ ☆ ☆ ☆   Difficulty: 1 2 3 4 5

Companions: _____

_____

_____

Favourite moment: _____

_____

_____

Notes: _____

_____

_____

_____

_____

_____

_____

_____

_____

_____

_____

Saileag
956m

Date: _____ Weather: _____ Temperature: _____

Start time: _____ End time: _____ Total distance: _____

Climb rating: ☆ ☆ ☆ ☆ ☆   Difficulty: 1 2 3 4 5

Companions: _____

_____

_____

Favourite moment: _____

_____

_____

Notes: _____

_____

_____

_____

_____

_____

_____

_____

_____

Sgurr nan Coireachan (Finnan)
956m

Date: _____ Weather: _____ Temperature: _____

Start time: _____ End time: _____ Total distance: _____

Climb rating: ☆ ☆ ☆ ☆ ☆   Difficulty: 1 2 3 4 5

Companions: _____

_____

_____

Favourite moment: _____

_____

_____

Notes: _____

_____

_____

_____

_____

_____

_____

_____

_____

_____

Carn Ghluasaid
957m

Date: _____ Weather: _____ Temperature: _____

Start time: _____ End time: _____ Total distance: _____

Climb rating: ☆ ☆ ☆ ☆ ☆   Difficulty: 1 2 3 4 5

Companions: _____

_____

_____

Favourite moment: _____

_____

_____

Notes: _____

_____

_____

_____

_____

_____

_____

_____

_____

Tom Buidhe
957m

Date: _____ Weather: _____ Temperature: _____

Start time: _____ End time: _____ Total distance: _____

Climb rating: ☆ ☆ ☆ ☆ ☆   Difficulty: 1 2 3 4 5

Companions: _____

_____

_____

Favourite moment: _____

_____

_____

Notes: _____

_____

_____

_____

_____

_____

_____

_____

_____

_____

Tolmount
958m

Date: _____ Weather: _____ Temperature: _____

Start time: _____ End time: _____ Total distance: _____

Climb rating: ☆ ☆ ☆ ☆ ☆   Difficulty: 1 2 3 4 5

Companions: _____

_____

_____

Favourite moment: _____

_____

_____

Notes: _____

_____

_____

_____

_____

_____

_____

_____

Etive Beag - Stob Dubh
958m

Date: _____ Weather: _____ Temperature: _____

Start time: _____ End time: _____ Total distance: _____

Climb rating: ☆ ☆ ☆ ☆ ☆   Difficulty: 1 2 3 4 5

Companions: _____

_____

_____

Favourite moment: _____

_____

_____

Notes: _____

_____

_____

_____

_____

_____

_____

_____

_____

_____

_____

Bruach na Frithe
959m

Date: _____ Weather: _____ Temperature: _____

Start time: _____ End time: _____ Total distance: _____

Climb rating: ☆ ☆ ☆ ☆ ☆   Difficulty: 1 2 3 4 5

Companions: _____

_____

_____

Favourite moment: _____

_____

_____

Notes: _____

_____

_____

_____

_____

_____

_____

_____

_____

Beinn Fhionnlaidh (Etive)
959m

Date: _____ Weather: _____ Temperature: _____

Start time: _____ End time: _____ Total distance: _____

Climb rating: ☆ ☆ ☆ ☆ ☆ Difficulty: 1 2 3 4 5

Companions: _____

_____

_____

Favourite moment: _____

_____

_____

Notes: _____

_____

_____

_____

_____

_____

_____

_____

_____

_____

Meall Glas (Loch Tay)
959m

Date: _____ Weather: _____ Temperature: _____

Start time: _____ End time: _____ Total distance: _____

Climb rating: ☆ ☆ ☆ ☆ ☆   Difficulty: 1 2 3 4 5

Companions: _____

_____

_____

Favourite moment: _____

_____

_____

Notes: _____

_____

_____

_____

_____

_____

_____

_____

_____

_____

Beinn nan Aighenan
960m

Date: _____ Weather: _____ Temperature: _____

Start time: _____ End time: _____ Total distance: _____

Climb rating: ☆ ☆ ☆ ☆ ☆   Difficulty: 1 2 3 4 5

Companions: _____

_____

_____

Favourite moment: _____

_____

_____

Notes: _____

_____

_____

_____

_____

_____

_____

_____

_____

_____

Stuchd an Lochain
960m

Date: _____ Weather: _____ Temperature: _____

Start time: _____ End time: _____ Total distance: _____

Climb rating: ☆ ☆ ☆ ☆ ☆   Difficulty: 1 2 3 4 5

Companions: _____

_____

_____

Favourite moment: _____

_____

_____

Notes: _____

_____

_____

_____

_____

_____

_____

_____

_____

Sgurr Ruadh
961m

Date: _____ Weather: _____ Temperature: _____

Start time: _____ End time: _____ Total distance: _____

Climb rating: ☆ ☆ ☆ ☆ ☆   Difficulty: 1 2 3 4 5

Companions: _____

_____

_____

Favourite moment: _____

_____

_____

Notes: _____

_____

_____

_____

_____

_____

_____

_____

_____

_____

Ben Klibreck
962m

Date: _____ Weather: _____ Temperature: _____

Start time: _____ End time: _____ Total distance: _____

Climb rating: ☆ ☆ ☆ ☆ ☆   Difficulty: 1 2 3 4 5

Companions: _____

_____

_____

Favourite moment: _____

_____

_____

Notes: _____

_____

_____

_____

_____

_____

_____

_____

_____

_____

Sgurr Thuilm
963m

Date: _____   Weather: _____   Temperature: _____

Start time: _____   End time: _____   Total distance: _____

Climb rating: ☆ ☆ ☆ ☆ ☆   Difficulty: 1 2 3 4 5

Companions: _____

_____

_____

Favourite moment: _____

_____

_____

Notes: _____

_____

_____

_____

_____

_____

_____

_____

_____

_____

Carn a' Chlamain
964m

Date: _____ Weather: _____ Temperature: _____

Start time: _____ End time: _____ Total distance: _____

Climb rating: ☆ ☆ ☆ ☆ ☆   Difficulty: 1 2 3 4 5

Companions: _____

_____

_____

Favourite moment: _____

_____

_____

Notes: _____

_____

_____

_____

_____

_____

_____

_____

_____

Sgurr na Banachdich
965m

Date: _____ Weather: _____ Temperature: _____

Start time: _____ End time: _____ Total distance: _____

Climb rating: ☆ ☆ ☆ ☆ ☆   Difficulty: 1 2 3 4 5

Companions: _____

_____

_____

Favourite moment: _____

_____

_____

Notes: _____

_____

_____

_____

_____

_____

_____

_____

_____

_____

Ben More (Mull)
966m

Date: _____ Weather: _____ Temperature: _____

Start time: _____ End time: _____ Total distance: _____

Climb rating: ☆ ☆ ☆ ☆ ☆   Difficulty: 1 2 3 4 5

Companions: _____

_____

_____

Favourite moment: _____

_____

_____

Notes: _____

_____

_____

_____

_____

_____

_____

_____

_____

_____

Sgurr nan Gilean
966m

Date: _____ Weather: _____ Temperature: _____

Start time: _____ End time: _____ Total distance: _____

Climb rating: ☆ ☆ ☆ ☆ ☆   Difficulty: 1 2 3 4 5

Companions: _____

_____

_____

Favourite moment: _____

_____

_____

Notes: _____

_____

_____

_____

_____

_____

_____

_____

_____

_____

A' Mhaighdean
967m

Date: _____ Weather: _____ Temperature: _____

Start time: _____ End time: _____ Total distance: _____

Climb rating: ☆ ☆ ☆ ☆ ☆   Difficulty: 1 2 3 4 5

Companions: _____

_____

_____

Favourite moment: _____

_____

_____

Notes: _____

_____

_____

_____

_____

_____

_____

_____

_____

Aonach Eagach - Sgorr nam Fiannaidh
968m

Date: _____ Weather: _____ Temperature: _____

Start time: _____ End time: _____ Total distance: _____

Climb rating: ☆ ☆ ☆ ☆ ☆   Difficulty: 1 2 3 4 5

Companions: _____

_____

_____

Favourite moment: _____

_____

_____

Notes: _____

_____

_____

_____

_____

_____

_____

_____

_____

_____

_____

Meall Garbh (Lyon)
968m

Date: _____ Weather: _____ Temperature: _____

Start time: _____ End time: _____ Total distance: _____

Climb rating: ☆ ☆ ☆ ☆ ☆   Difficulty: 1 2 3 4 5

Companions: _____

_____

_____

Favourite moment: _____

_____

_____

Notes: _____

_____

_____

_____

_____

_____

_____

_____

Sgurr a' Ghreadaidh
972m

Date: _____ Weather: _____ Temperature: _____

Start time: _____ End time: _____ Total distance: _____

Climb rating: ☆ ☆ ☆ ☆ ☆   Difficulty: 1 2 3 4 5

Companions: _____

_____

_____

Favourite moment: _____

_____

_____

Notes: _____

_____

_____

_____

_____

_____

_____

_____

_____

A' Mharconaich
973m

Date: _____ Weather: _____ Temperature: _____

Start time: _____ End time: _____ Total distance: _____

Climb rating: ☆ ☆ ☆ ☆ ☆   Difficulty: 1 2 3 4 5

Companions: _____

_____

_____

Favourite moment: _____

_____

_____

Notes: _____

_____

_____

_____

_____

_____

_____

_____

_____

_____

Beinn Sgritheall
974m

Date: _____ Weather: _____ Temperature: _____

Start time: _____ End time: _____ Total distance: _____

Climb rating: ☆ ☆ ☆ ☆ ☆   Difficulty: 1 2 3 4 5

Companions: _____

_____

_____

Favourite moment: _____

_____

_____

Notes: _____

_____

_____

_____

_____

_____

_____

_____

_____

Ben Lamond
974m

Date: _____ Weather: _____ Temperature: _____

Start time: _____ End time: _____ Total distance: _____

Climb rating: ☆ ☆ ☆ ☆ ☆   Difficulty: 1 2 3 4 5

Companions: _____

_____

_____

Favourite moment: _____

_____

_____

Notes: _____

_____

_____

_____

_____

_____

_____

_____

_____

_____

Carn a' Gheoidh
975m

Date: _____ Weather: _____ Temperature: _____

Start time: _____ End time: _____ Total distance: _____

Climb rating: ☆ ☆ ☆ ☆ ☆   Difficulty: 1 2 3 4 5

Companions: _____

_____

_____

Favourite moment: _____

_____

_____

Notes: _____

_____

_____

_____

_____

_____

_____

_____

_____

_____

Stuc a' Chroin
975m

Date: _____ Weather: _____ Temperature: _____

Start time: _____ End time: _____ Total distance: _____

Climb rating: ☆ ☆ ☆ ☆ ☆   Difficulty: 1 2 3 4 5

Companions: _____

_____

_____

Favourite moment: _____

_____

_____

Notes: _____

_____

_____

_____

_____

_____

_____

_____

_____

_____

Beinn a' Ghlo - Carn Liath
976m

Date: _____ Weather: _____ Temperature: _____

Start time: _____ End time: _____ Total distance: _____

Climb rating: ☆ ☆ ☆ ☆ ☆   Difficulty: 1 2 3 4 5

Companions: _____

_____

_____

Favourite moment: _____

_____

_____

Notes: _____

_____

_____

_____

_____

_____

_____

_____

_____

_____

Meall nan Ceapraichean
977m

Date: _____ Weather: _____ Temperature: _____

Start time: _____ End time: _____ Total distance: _____

Climb rating: ☆ ☆ ☆ ☆ ☆   Difficulty: 1 2 3 4 5

Companions: _____

_____

_____

Favourite moment: _____

_____

_____

Notes: _____

_____

_____

_____

_____

_____

_____

_____

_____

_____

Stob Ban (Grey Corries)
977m

Date: _____ Weather: _____ Temperature: _____

Start time: _____ End time: _____ Total distance: _____

Climb rating: ☆ ☆ ☆ ☆ ☆   Difficulty: 1 2 3 4 5

Companions: _____

_____

_____

Favourite moment: _____

_____

_____

Notes: _____

_____

_____

_____

_____

_____

_____

_____

_____

_____

Cona' Mheall
978m

Date: _____ Weather: _____ Temperature: _____

Start time: _____ End time: _____ Total distance: _____

Climb rating: ☆ ☆ ☆ ☆ ☆   Difficulty: 1 2 3 4 5

Companions: _____

_____

_____

Favourite moment: _____

_____

_____

Notes: _____

_____

_____

_____

_____

_____

_____

_____

_____

_____

Beinn Dubhchraig
978m

Date: _____ Weather: _____ Temperature: _____

Start time: _____ End time: _____ Total distance: _____

Climb rating: ☆ ☆ ☆ ☆ ☆   Difficulty: 1 2 3 4 5

Companions: _____

_____

_____

Favourite moment: _____

_____

_____

Notes: _____

_____

_____

_____

_____

_____

_____

_____

_____

Stob Coire Sgriodain
979m

Date: _____ Weather: _____ Temperature: _____

Start time: _____ End time: _____ Total distance: _____

Climb rating: ☆ ☆ ☆ ☆ ☆   Difficulty: 1 2 3 4 5

Companions: _____

_____

_____

Favourite moment: _____

_____

_____

Notes: _____

_____

_____

_____

_____

_____

_____

_____

_____

_____

Beinn a' Chochuill
980m

Date: _____ Weather: _____ Temperature: _____

Start time: _____ End time: _____ Total distance: _____

Climb rating: ☆ ☆ ☆ ☆ ☆   Difficulty: 1 2 3 4 5

Companions: _____

_____

_____

Favourite moment: _____

_____

_____

Notes: _____

_____

_____

_____

_____

_____

_____

_____

_____

_____

Maol Chinn-dearg (Shiel)
980m

Date: _____ Weather: _____ Temperature: _____

Start time: _____ End time: _____ Total distance: _____

Climb rating: ☆ ☆ ☆ ☆ ☆   Difficulty: 1 2 3 4 5

Companions: _____

_____

_____

Favourite moment: _____

_____

_____

Notes: _____

_____

_____

_____

_____

_____

_____

_____

_____

_____

Slioch
981m

Date: _____ Weather: _____ Temperature: _____

Start time: _____ End time: _____ Total distance: _____

Climb rating: ☆ ☆ ☆ ☆ ☆   Difficulty: 1 2 3 4 5

Companions: _____

_____

_____

Favourite moment: _____

_____

_____

Notes: _____

_____

_____

_____

_____

_____

_____

_____

_____

_____

Meall na Aighean
981m

Date: _____ Weather: _____ Temperature: _____

Start time: _____ End time: _____ Total distance: _____

Climb rating: ☆ ☆ ☆ ☆ ☆   Difficulty: 1 2 3 4 5

Companions: _____

_____

_____

Favourite moment: _____

_____

_____

Notes: _____

_____

_____

_____

_____

_____

_____

_____

_____

_____

Ciste Dhubh
981m

Date: _____ Weather: _____ Temperature: _____

Start time: _____ End time: _____ Total distance: _____

Climb rating: ☆ ☆ ☆ ☆ ☆   Difficulty: 1 2 3 4 5

Companions: _____

_____

_____

Favourite moment: _____

_____

_____

Notes: _____

_____

_____

_____

_____

_____

_____

_____

_____

Stob Coire a' Chairn
981m

Date: _____ Weather: _____ Temperature: _____

Start time: _____ End time: _____ Total distance: _____

Climb rating: ☆ ☆ ☆ ☆ ☆   Difficulty: 1 2 3 4 5

Companions: _____

_____

_____

Favourite moment: _____

_____

_____

Notes: _____

_____

_____

_____

_____

_____

_____

_____

_____

_____

An Gearanach
982m

Date: _____ Weather: _____ Temperature: _____

Start time: _____ End time: _____ Total distance: _____

Climb rating: ☆ ☆ ☆ ☆ ☆   Difficulty: 1 2 3 4 5

Companions: _____

_____

_____

Favourite moment: _____

_____

_____

Notes: _____

_____

_____

_____

_____

_____

_____

_____

_____

_____

Mullach na Dheiragain
982m

Date: _____ Weather: _____ Temperature: _____

Start time: _____ End time: _____ Total distance: _____

Climb rating: ☆ ☆ ☆ ☆ ☆   Difficulty: 1 2 3 4 5

Companions: _____

_____

_____

Favourite moment: _____

_____

_____

Notes: _____

_____

_____

_____

_____

_____

_____

_____

_____

Ben Vorlich
985m

Date: _____   Weather: _____   Temperature: _____

Start time: _____   End time: _____   Total distance: _____

Climb rating: ☆ ☆ ☆ ☆ ☆   Difficulty: 1 2 3 4 5

Companions: _____

_____

_____

Favourite moment: _____

_____

_____

Notes: _____

_____

_____

_____

_____

_____

_____

_____

_____

_____

Sgurr Dearg - Inaccessible Pinnacle
986m

Date: _____ Weather: _____ Temperature: _____

Start time: _____ End time: _____ Total distance: _____

Climb rating: ☆ ☆ ☆ ☆ ☆   Difficulty: 1 2 3 4 5

Companions: _____

_____

_____

Favourite moment: _____

_____

_____

Notes: _____

_____

_____

_____

_____

_____

_____

_____

_____

Beinne Alligin - Sgurr Mhor
986m

Date: _____ Weather: _____ Temperature: _____

Start time: _____ End time: _____ Total distance: _____

Climb rating: ☆ ☆ ☆ ☆ ☆   Difficulty: 1 2 3 4 5

Companions: _____

_____

_____

Favourite moment: _____

_____

_____

Notes: _____

_____

_____

_____

_____

_____

_____

_____

_____

Conival (Cona' Mheall)
987m

Date: _____ Weather: _____ Temperature: _____

Start time: _____ End time: _____ Total distance: _____

Climb rating: ☆ ☆ ☆ ☆ ☆   Difficulty: 1 2 3 4 5

Companions: _____

_____

_____

Favourite moment: _____

_____

_____

Notes: _____

_____

_____

_____

_____

_____

_____

_____

_____

Lurg Mhor
987m

Date: _____ Weather: _____ Temperature: _____

Start time: _____ End time: _____ Total distance: _____

Climb rating: ☆ ☆ ☆ ☆ ☆   Difficulty: 1 2 3 4 5

Companions: _____

_____

_____

Favourite moment: _____

_____

_____

Notes: _____

_____

_____

_____

_____

_____

_____

_____

_____

_____

Gaor Bheinn (Gulvain)
987m

Date: _____ Weather: _____ Temperature: _____

Start time: _____ End time: _____ Total distance: _____

Climb rating: ☆ ☆ ☆ ☆ ☆ Difficulty: 1 2 3 4 5

Companions: _____

_____

_____

Favourite moment: _____

_____

_____

Notes: _____

_____

_____

_____

_____

_____

_____

_____

_____

Druim Shionnach
987m

Date: _____ Weather: _____ Temperature: _____

Start time: _____ End time: _____ Total distance: _____

Climb rating: ☆ ☆ ☆ ☆ ☆   Difficulty: 1 2 3 4 5

Companions: _____

_____

_____

Favourite moment: _____

_____

_____

Notes: _____

_____

_____

_____

_____

_____

_____

_____

_____

_____

Creag Leacach
988m

Date: _____ Weather: _____ Temperature: _____

Start time: _____ End time: _____ Total distance: _____

Climb rating: ☆ ☆ ☆ ☆ ☆   Difficulty: 1 2 3 4 5

Companions: _____

_____

_____

Favourite moment: _____

_____

_____

Notes: _____

_____

_____

_____

_____

_____

_____

_____

_____

_____

Sgurr Ban (Fisherfield)
989m

Date: _____ Weather: _____ Temperature: _____

Start time: _____ End time: _____ Total distance: _____

Climb rating: ☆ ☆ ☆ ☆ ☆   Difficulty: 1 2 3 4 5

Companions: _____

_____

_____

Favourite moment: _____

_____

_____

Notes: _____

_____

_____

_____

_____

_____

_____

_____

_____

_____

_____

Beinn Eunaich
989m

Date: _____ Weather: _____ Temperature: _____

Start time: _____ End time: _____ Total distance: _____

Climb rating: ☆ ☆ ☆ ☆ ☆   Difficulty: 1 2 3 4 5

Companions: _____

_____

_____

Favourite moment: _____

_____

_____

Notes: _____

_____

_____

_____

_____

_____

_____

_____

_____

Sgairneach Mhor
991m

Date: _____ Weather: _____ Temperature: _____

Start time: _____ End time: _____ Total distance: _____

Climb rating: ☆ ☆ ☆ ☆ ☆   Difficulty: 1 2 3 4 5

Companions: _____

_____

_____

Favourite moment: _____

_____

_____

Notes: _____

_____

_____

_____

_____

_____

_____

_____

_____

_____

_____

Sgurr Alasdair
992m

Date: _____ Weather: _____ Temperature: _____

Start time: _____ End time: _____ Total distance: _____

Climb rating: ☆ ☆ ☆ ☆ ☆   Difficulty: 1 2 3 4 5

Companions: _____

_____

_____

Favourite moment: _____

_____

_____

Notes: _____

_____

_____

_____

_____

_____

_____

_____

_____

Carn nan Gobhar (Strathfarrar)
993m

Date: _____ Weather: _____ Temperature: _____

Start time: _____ End time: _____ Total distance: _____

Climb rating: ☆ ☆ ☆ ☆ ☆   Difficulty: 1 2 3 4 5

Companions: _____

_____

_____

Favourite moment: _____

_____

_____

Notes: _____

_____

_____

_____

_____

_____

_____

_____

_____

Beinn Eighe - Spidean Coire nan Clach
993m

Date: _____ Weather: _____ Temperature: _____

Start time: _____ End time: _____ Total distance: _____

Climb rating: ☆ ☆ ☆ ☆ ☆   Difficulty: 1 2 3 4 5

Companions: _____

_____

_____

Favourite moment: _____

_____

_____

Notes: _____

_____

_____

_____

_____

_____

_____

_____

_____

Carn nan Gobhar (Cannich)
993m

Date: _____ Weather: _____ Temperature: _____

Start time: _____ End time: _____ Total distance: _____

Climb rating: ☆ ☆ ☆ ☆ ☆   Difficulty: 1 2 3 4 5

Companions: _____

_____

_____

Favourite moment: _____

_____

_____

Notes: _____

_____

_____

_____

_____

_____

_____

_____

_____

_____

Sgurr na Ruaidhe
993m

Date: _____   Weather: _____   Temperature: _____

Start time: _____   End time: _____   Total distance: _____

Climb rating: ☆ ☆ ☆ ☆ ☆   Difficulty: 1 2 3 4 5

Companions: _____

_____

_____

Favourite moment: _____

_____

_____

Notes: _____

_____

_____

_____

_____

_____

_____

_____

_____

_____

Sgurr na h-Ulaidh
994m

Date: _____ Weather: _____ Temperature: _____

Start time: _____ End time: _____ Total distance: _____

Climb rating: ☆ ☆ ☆ ☆ ☆   Difficulty: 1 2 3 4 5

Companions: _____

_____

_____

Favourite moment: _____

_____

_____

Notes: _____

_____

_____

_____

_____

_____

_____

_____

_____

_____

Carn an Fhidhleir (Carn Easlar)
994m

Date: _____ Weather: _____ Temperature: _____

Start time: _____ End time: _____ Total distance: _____

Climb rating: ☆ ☆ ☆ ☆ ☆   Difficulty: 1 2 3 4 5

Companions: _____

_____

_____

Favourite moment: _____

_____

_____

Notes: _____

_____

_____

_____

_____

_____

_____

_____

_____

An Caisteal
996m

Date: _____ Weather: _____ Temperature: _____

Start time: _____ End time: _____ Total distance: _____

Climb rating: ☆ ☆ ☆ ☆ ☆   Difficulty: 1 2 3 4 5

Companions: _____

_____

_____

Favourite moment: _____

_____

_____

Notes: _____

_____

_____

_____

_____

_____

_____

_____

_____

_____

_____

Spidean Mialach
996m

Date: _____ Weather: _____ Temperature: _____

Start time: _____ End time: _____ Total distance: _____

Climb rating: ☆ ☆ ☆ ☆ ☆   Difficulty: 1 2 3 4 5

Companions: _____

_____

_____

Favourite moment: _____

_____

_____

Notes: _____

_____

_____

_____

_____

_____

_____

_____

_____

A' Chailleach (Fannaichs)
997m

Date: _____ Weather: _____ Temperature: _____

Start time: _____ End time: _____ Total distance: _____

Climb rating: ☆ ☆ ☆ ☆ ☆ Difficulty: 1 2 3 4 5

Companions: _____

_____

_____

Favourite moment: _____

_____

_____

Notes: _____

_____

_____

_____

_____

_____

_____

_____

_____

Glas Bheinn Mhor
998m

Date: _____ Weather: _____ Temperature: _____

Start time: _____ End time: _____ Total distance: _____

Climb rating: ☆ ☆ ☆ ☆ ☆   Difficulty: 1 2 3 4 5

Companions: _____

_____

_____

Favourite moment: _____

_____

_____

Notes: _____

_____

_____

_____

_____

_____

_____

_____

_____

Ben More Assynt
998m

Date: _____ Weather: _____ Temperature: _____

Start time: _____ End time: _____ Total distance: _____

Climb rating: ☆ ☆ ☆ ☆ ☆   Difficulty: 1 2 3 4 5

Companions: _____

_____

_____

Favourite moment: _____

_____

_____

Notes: _____

_____

_____

_____

_____

_____

_____

_____

_____

_____

Broad Chairn
998m

Date: _____ Weather: _____ Temperature: _____

Start time: _____ End time: _____ Total distance: _____

Climb rating: ☆ ☆ ☆ ☆ ☆   Difficulty: 1 2 3 4 5

Companions: _____

_____

_____

Favourite moment: _____

_____

_____

Notes: _____

_____

_____

_____

_____

_____

_____

_____

_____

_____

Sgurr Breac
999m

Date: _____ Weather: _____ Temperature: _____

Start time: _____ End time: _____ Total distance: _____

Climb rating: ☆ ☆ ☆ ☆ ☆   Difficulty: 1 2 3 4 5

Companions: _____

_____

_____

Favourite moment: _____

_____

_____

Notes: _____

_____

_____

_____

_____

_____

_____

_____

_____

_____

Sgurr Choinnich
999m

Date: _____ Weather: _____ Temperature: _____

Start time: _____ End time: _____ Total distance: _____

Climb rating: ☆ ☆ ☆ ☆ ☆   Difficulty: 1 2 3 4 5

Companions: _____

_____

_____

Favourite moment: _____

_____

_____

Notes: _____

_____

_____

_____

_____

_____

_____

_____

_____

Stob Diamh
999m

Date: _____ Weather: _____ Temperature: _____

Start time: _____ End time: _____ Total distance: _____

Climb rating: ☆ ☆ ☆ ☆ ☆   Difficulty: 1 2 3 4 5

Companions: _____

_____

_____

Favourite moment: _____

_____

_____

Notes: _____

_____

_____

_____

_____

_____

_____

_____

_____

_____

Stob Ban (Mamores)
1,000m

Date: _____ Weather: _____ Temperature: _____

Start time: _____ End time: _____ Total distance: _____

Climb rating: ☆ ☆ ☆ ☆ ☆   Difficulty: 1 2 3 4 5

Companions: _____

_____

_____

Favourite moment: _____

_____

_____

Notes: _____

_____

_____

_____

_____

_____

_____

_____

_____

Aonach Meadhoin
1,001m

Date: _____ Weather: _____ Temperature: _____

Start time: _____ End time: _____ Total distance: _____

Climb rating: ☆ ☆ ☆ ☆ ☆   Difficulty: 1 2 3 4 5

Companions: _____

_____

_____

Favourite moment: _____

_____

_____

Notes: _____

_____

_____

_____

_____

_____

_____

_____

_____

_____

_____

Beinn a' Bheithir - Sgorr Dhonuill
1,001m

Date: _____ Weather: _____ Temperature: _____

Start time: _____ End time: _____ Total distance: _____

Climb rating: ☆ ☆ ☆ ☆ ☆   Difficulty: 1 2 3 4 5

Companions: _____

_____

_____

Favourite moment: _____

_____

_____

Notes: _____

_____

_____

_____

_____

_____

_____

_____

_____

_____

Meall Greigh
1,001m

Date: _____ Weather: _____ Temperature: _____

Start time: _____ End time: _____ Total distance: _____

Climb rating: ☆ ☆ ☆ ☆ ☆   Difficulty: 1 2 3 4 5

Companions: _____

_____

_____

Favourite moment: _____

_____

_____

Notes: _____

_____

_____

_____

_____

_____

_____

_____

_____

_____

Sail Chaorainn
1,002m

Date: _____ Weather: _____ Temperature: _____

Start time: _____ End time: _____ Total distance: _____

Climb rating: ☆ ☆ ☆ ☆ ☆ Difficulty: 1 2 3 4 5

Companions: _____

_____

_____

Favourite moment: _____

_____

_____

Notes: _____

_____

_____

_____

_____

_____

_____

_____

_____

_____

_____

Sgurr na Carnach
1,002m

Date: _____ Weather: _____ Temperature: _____

Start time: _____ End time: _____ Total distance: _____

Climb rating: ☆ ☆ ☆ ☆ ☆   Difficulty: 1 2 3 4 5

Companions: _____

_____

_____

Favourite moment: _____

_____

_____

Notes: _____

_____

_____

_____

_____

_____

_____

_____

_____

_____

_____

Sgurr Mor (Glen Kingie)
1,003m

Date: _____ Weather: _____ Temperature: _____

Start time: _____ End time: _____ Total distance: _____

Climb rating: ☆ ☆ ☆ ☆ ☆   Difficulty: 1 2 3 4 5

Companions: _____

_____

_____

Favourite moment: _____

_____

_____

Notes: _____

_____

_____

_____

_____

_____

_____

_____

_____

_____

Sgurr an Lochain
1,004m

Date: _____ Weather: _____ Temperature: _____

Start time: _____ End time: _____ Total distance: _____

Climb rating: ☆ ☆ ☆ ☆ ☆   Difficulty: 1 2 3 4 5

Companions: _____

_____

_____

Favourite moment: _____

_____

_____

Notes: _____

_____

_____

_____

_____

_____

_____

_____

_____

_____

_____

The Devil's Point
1,004m

Date: _____ Weather: _____ Temperature: _____

Start time: _____ End time: _____ Total distance: _____

Climb rating: ☆ ☆ ☆ ☆ ☆   Difficulty: 1 2 3 4 5

Companions: _____

_____

_____

Favourite moment: _____

_____

_____

Notes: _____

_____

_____

_____

_____

_____

_____

_____

_____

Beinn an Dothaidh
1,004m

Date: _____ Weather: _____ Temperature: _____

Start time: _____ End time: _____ Total distance: _____

Climb rating: ☆ ☆ ☆ ☆ ☆   Difficulty: 1 2 3 4 5

Companions: _____

_____

_____

Favourite moment: _____

_____

_____

Notes: _____

_____

_____

_____

_____

_____

_____

_____

_____

_____

Beinn Fhionnlaidh (Cannich)
1,005m

Date: _____ Weather: _____ Temperature: _____

Start time: _____ End time: _____ Total distance: _____

Climb rating: ☆ ☆ ☆ ☆ ☆   Difficulty: 1 2 3 4 5

Companions: _____

_____

_____

Favourite moment: _____

_____

_____

Notes: _____

_____

_____

_____

_____

_____

_____

_____

_____

Maoile Lunndaidh
1,005m

Date: _____ Weather: _____ Temperature: _____

Start time: _____ End time: _____ Total distance: _____

Climb rating: ☆ ☆ ☆ ☆ ☆   Difficulty: 1 2 3 4 5

Companions: _____

_____

_____

Favourite moment: _____

_____

_____

Notes: _____

_____

_____

_____

_____

_____

_____

_____

_____

_____

_____

Carn Liath (Meagaidh)
1,006m

Date: _____ Weather: _____ Temperature: _____

Start time: _____ End time: _____ Total distance: _____

Climb rating: ☆ ☆ ☆ ☆ ☆   Difficulty: 1 2 3 4 5

Companions: _____

_____

_____

Favourite moment: _____

_____

_____

Notes: _____

_____

_____

_____

_____

_____

_____

_____

_____

An Sgarsoch
1,007m

Date: _____ Weather: _____ Temperature: _____

Start time: _____ End time: _____ Total distance: _____

Climb rating: ☆ ☆ ☆ ☆ ☆   Difficulty: 1 2 3 4 5

Companions: _____

_____

_____

Favourite moment: _____

_____

_____

Notes: _____

_____

_____

_____

_____

_____

_____

_____

_____

_____

Beinn Dearg (Bruar)
1,009m

Date: _____ Weather: _____ Temperature: _____

Start time: _____ End time: _____ Total distance: _____

Climb rating: ☆ ☆ ☆ ☆ ☆   Difficulty: 1 2 3 4 5

Companions: _____

_____

_____

Favourite moment: _____

_____

_____

Notes: _____

_____

_____

_____

_____

_____

_____

_____

_____

_____

Beinn Eigh - Ruadh-stac Mor
1,010m

Date: _____ Weather: _____ Temperature: _____

Start time: _____ End time: _____ Total distance: _____

Climb rating: ☆ ☆ ☆ ☆ ☆   Difficulty: 1 2 3 4 5

Companions: _____

_____

_____

Favourite moment: _____

_____

_____

Notes: _____

_____

_____

_____

_____

_____

_____

_____

_____

_____

Sgurr an Doire Leathain
1,010m

Date: _____ Weather: _____ Temperature: _____

Start time: _____ End time: _____ Total distance: _____

Climb rating: ☆ ☆ ☆ ☆ ☆   Difficulty: 1 2 3 4 5

Companions: _____

_____

_____

Favourite moment: _____

_____

_____

Notes: _____

_____

_____

_____

_____

_____

_____

_____

_____

_____

Sgurr Eilde Mor
1,010m

Date: _____ Weather: _____ Temperature: _____

Start time: _____ End time: _____ Total distance: _____

Climb rating: ☆ ☆ ☆ ☆ ☆   Difficulty: 1 2 3 4 5

Companions: _____

_____

_____

Favourite moment: _____

_____

_____

Notes: _____

_____

_____

_____

_____

_____

_____

_____

_____

_____

Beinn Udlamain
1,010m

Date: _____ Weather: _____ Temperature: _____

Start time: _____ End time: _____ Total distance: _____

Climb rating: ☆ ☆ ☆ ☆ ☆   Difficulty: 1 2 3 4 5

Companions: _____

_____

_____

Favourite moment: _____

_____

_____

Notes: _____

_____

_____

_____

_____

_____

_____

_____

_____

The Saddle
1,011m

Date: _____   Weather: _____   Temperature: _____

Start time: _____   End time: _____   Total distance: _____

Climb rating: ☆ ☆ ☆ ☆ ☆   Difficulty: 1 2 3 4 5

Companions: _____

_____

_____

Favourite moment: _____

_____

_____

Notes: _____

_____

_____

_____

_____

_____

_____

_____

_____

_____

Cairn Bannoch
1,012m

Date: _____ Weather: _____ Temperature: _____

Start time: _____ End time: _____ Total distance: _____

Climb rating: ☆ ☆ ☆ ☆ ☆   Difficulty: 1 2 3 4 5

Companions: _____

_____

_____

Favourite moment: _____

_____

_____

Notes: _____

_____

_____

_____

_____

_____

_____

_____

_____

Beinn Ime
1,012m

Date: _____ Weather: _____ Temperature: _____

Start time: _____ End time: _____ Total distance: _____

Climb rating: ☆ ☆ ☆ ☆ ☆   Difficulty: 1 2 3 4 5

Companions: _____

_____

_____

Favourite moment: _____

_____

_____

Notes: _____

_____

_____

_____

_____

_____

_____

_____

_____

_____

Garbh Chioch Mhor
1,013m

Date: _____ Weather: _____ Temperature: _____

Start time: _____ End time: _____ Total distance: _____

Climb rating: ☆ ☆ ☆ ☆ ☆ Difficulty: 1 2 3 4 5

Companions: _____

_____

_____

Favourite moment: _____

_____

_____

Notes: _____

_____

_____

_____

_____

_____

_____

_____

_____

Mullach Coire Mhic Fhearchair
1,015m

Date: _____ Weather: _____ Temperature: _____

Start time: _____ End time: _____ Total distance: _____

Climb rating: ☆ ☆ ☆ ☆ ☆   Difficulty: 1 2 3 4 5

Companions: _____

_____

_____

Favourite moment: _____

_____

_____

Notes: _____

_____

_____

_____

_____

_____

_____

_____

_____

Mullach Clach a' Bhlair
1,019m

Date: _____   Weather: _____   Temperature: _____

Start time: _____   End time: _____   Total distance: _____

Climb rating: ☆ ☆ ☆ ☆ ☆   Difficulty: 1 2 3 4 5

Companions: _____

_____

_____

Favourite moment: _____

_____

_____

Notes: _____

_____

_____

_____

_____

_____

_____

_____

_____

_____

Carn an Tuirc
1,019m

Date: _____ Weather: _____ Temperature: _____

Start time: _____ End time: _____ Total distance: _____

Climb rating: ☆ ☆ ☆ ☆ ☆   Difficulty: 1 2 3 4 5

Companions: _____

_____

_____

Favourite moment: _____

_____

_____

Notes: _____

_____

_____

_____

_____

_____

_____

_____

_____

_____

_____

Beinn Bheoil
1,019m

Date: _____ Weather: _____ Temperature: _____

Start time: _____ End time: _____ Total distance: _____

Climb rating: ☆ ☆ ☆ ☆ ☆   Difficulty: 1 2 3 4 5

Companions: _____

_____

_____

Favourite moment: _____

_____

_____

Notes: _____

_____

_____

_____

_____

_____

_____

_____

_____

_____

Aonach air Chrith
1,020m

Date: _____ Weather: _____ Temperature: _____

Start time: _____ End time: _____ Total distance: _____

Climb rating: ☆ ☆ ☆ ☆ ☆   Difficulty: 1 2 3 4 5

Companions: _____

_____

_____

Favourite moment: _____

_____

_____

Notes: _____

_____

_____

_____

_____

_____

_____

_____

_____

_____

Ladhar Bheinn
1,020m

Date: _____ Weather: _____ Temperature: _____

Start time: _____ End time: _____ Total distance: _____

Climb rating: ☆ ☆ ☆ ☆ ☆   Difficulty: 1 2 3 4 5

Companions: _____

_____

_____

Favourite moment: _____

_____

_____

Notes: _____

_____

_____

_____

_____

_____

_____

_____

_____

_____

Etive Mor - Stob Dearg
1,021m

Date: _____ Weather: _____ Temperature: _____

Start time: _____ End time: _____ Total distance: _____

Climb rating: ☆ ☆ ☆ ☆ ☆   Difficulty: 1 2 3 4 5

Companions: _____

_____

_____

Favourite moment: _____

_____

_____

Notes: _____

_____

_____

_____

_____

_____

_____

_____

_____

_____

_____

Liatach Mullach an Rathain
1,024m

Date: _____ Weather: _____ Temperature: _____

Start time: _____ End time: _____ Total distance: _____

Climb rating: ☆ ☆ ☆ ☆ ☆   Difficulty: 1 2 3 4 5

Companions: _____

_____

_____

Favourite moment: _____

_____

_____

Notes: _____

_____

_____

_____

_____

_____

_____

_____

_____

Beinn a' Bheithir - Sgorr Dhearg
1,024m

Date: _____ Weather: _____ Temperature: _____

Start time: _____ End time: _____ Total distance: _____

Climb rating: ☆ ☆ ☆ ☆ ☆   Difficulty: 1 2 3 4 5

Companions: _____

_____

_____

Favourite moment: _____

_____

_____

Notes: _____

_____

_____

_____

_____

_____

_____

_____

_____

_____

_____

Ben Challum
1,025m

Date: _____ Weather: _____ Temperature: _____

Start time: _____ End time: _____ Total distance: _____

Climb rating: ☆ ☆ ☆ ☆ ☆   Difficulty: 1 2 3 4 5

Companions: _____

_____

_____

Favourite moment: _____

_____

_____

Notes: _____

_____

_____

_____

_____

_____

_____

_____

_____

Sgurr na Ciste Duibhe
1,027m

Date: _____ Weather: _____ Temperature: _____

Start time: _____ End time: _____ Total distance: _____

Climb rating: ☆ ☆ ☆ ☆ ☆   Difficulty: 1 2 3 4 5

Companions: _____

_____

_____

Favourite moment: _____

_____

_____

Notes: _____

_____

_____

_____

_____

_____

_____

_____

_____

_____

_____

Sgurr a' Mhaoraich
1,027m

Date: _____ Weather: _____ Temperature: _____

Start time: _____ End time: _____ Total distance: _____

Climb rating: ☆ ☆ ☆ ☆ ☆   Difficulty: 1 2 3 4 5

Companions: _____

_____

_____

Favourite moment: _____

_____

_____

Notes: _____

_____

_____

_____

_____

_____

_____

_____

_____

_____

Carn an Righ
1,029m

Date: _____ Weather: _____ Temperature: _____

Start time: _____ End time: _____ Total distance: _____

Climb rating: ☆ ☆ ☆ ☆ ☆   Difficulty: 1 2 3 4 5

Companions: _____

_____

_____

Favourite moment: _____

_____

_____

Notes: _____

_____

_____

_____

_____

_____

_____

_____

_____

_____

_____

Carn Gorm
1,029m

Date: _____ Weather: _____ Temperature: _____

Start time: _____ End time: _____ Total distance: _____

Climb rating: ☆ ☆ ☆ ☆ ☆   Difficulty: 1 2 3 4 5

Companions: _____

_____

_____

Favourite moment: _____

_____

_____

Notes: _____

_____

_____

_____

_____

_____

_____

_____

_____

Ben Oss
1,029m

Date: _____ Weather: _____ Temperature: _____

Start time: _____ End time: _____ Total distance: _____

Climb rating: ☆ ☆ ☆ ☆ ☆   Difficulty: 1 2 3 4 5

Companions: _____

_____

_____

Favourite moment: _____

_____

_____

Notes: _____

_____

_____

_____

_____

_____

_____

_____

_____

_____

Am Bodach
1,032m

Date: _____ Weather: _____ Temperature: _____

Start time: _____ End time: _____ Total distance: _____

Climb rating: ☆ ☆ ☆ ☆ ☆   Difficulty: 1 2 3 4 5

Companions: _____

_____

_____

Favourite moment: _____

_____

_____

Notes: _____

_____

_____

_____

_____

_____

_____

_____

_____

Beinn Fhada (Ben Attow)
1,032m

Date: _____ Weather: _____ Temperature: _____

Start time: _____ End time: _____ Total distance: _____

Climb rating: ☆ ☆ ☆ ☆ ☆　　Difficulty:　1　2　3　4　5

Companions: _____

_____

_____

Favourite moment: _____

_____

_____

Notes: _____

_____

_____

_____

_____

_____

_____

_____

Carn Dearg (Alder)
1,034m

Date: _____ Weather: _____ Temperature: _____

Start time: _____ End time: _____ Total distance: _____

Climb rating: ☆ ☆ ☆ ☆ ☆   Difficulty: 1 2 3 4 5

Companions: _____

_____

_____

Favourite moment: _____

_____

_____

Notes: _____

_____

_____

_____

_____

_____

_____

_____

_____

Gleouraich
1,035m

Date: _____ Weather: _____ Temperature: _____

Start time: _____ End time: _____ Total distance: _____

Climb rating: ☆ ☆ ☆ ☆ ☆   Difficulty: 1 2 3 4 5

Companions: _____

_____

_____

Favourite moment: _____

_____

_____

Notes: _____

_____

_____

_____

_____

_____

_____

_____

_____

_____

_____

Sgur a' Bhealaich Dheirg
1,036m

Date: _____ Weather: _____ Temperature: _____

Start time: _____ End time: _____ Total distance: _____

Climb rating: ☆ ☆ ☆ ☆ ☆   Difficulty: 1 2 3 4 5

Companions: _____

_____

_____

Favourite moment: _____

_____

_____

Notes: _____

_____

_____

_____

_____

_____

_____

_____

_____

Carn a' Mhaim
1,037m

Date: _____ Weather: _____ Temperature: _____

Start time: _____ End time: _____ Total distance: _____

Climb rating: ☆ ☆ ☆ ☆ ☆   Difficulty: 1 2 3 4 5

Companions: _____

_____

_____

Favourite moment: _____

_____

_____

Notes: _____

_____

_____

_____

_____

_____

_____

_____

_____

_____

_____

Beinn Achaladair
1,039m

Date: _____ Weather: _____ Temperature: _____

Start time: _____ End time: _____ Total distance: _____

Climb rating: ☆ ☆ ☆ ☆ ☆   Difficulty: 1 2 3 4 5

Companions: _____

_____

_____

Favourite moment: _____

_____

_____

Notes: _____

_____

_____

_____

_____

_____

_____

_____

_____

_____

Meall Ghaordaidh
1,040m

Date: _____ Weather: _____ Temperature: _____

Start time: _____ End time: _____ Total distance: _____

Climb rating: ☆ ☆ ☆ ☆ ☆   Difficulty: 1 2 3 4 5

Companions: _____

_____

_____

Favourite moment: _____

_____

_____

Notes: _____

_____

_____

_____

_____

_____

_____

_____

_____

Sgurr na Ciche
1,040m

Date: _____ Weather: _____ Temperature: _____

Start time: _____ End time: _____ Total distance: _____

Climb rating: ☆ ☆ ☆ ☆ ☆   Difficulty: 1 2 3 4 5

Companions: _____

_____

_____

Favourite moment: _____

_____

_____

Notes: _____

_____

_____

_____

_____

_____

_____

_____

_____

Carn Mairg
1,042m

Date: _____ Weather: _____ Temperature: _____

Start time: _____ End time: _____ Total distance: _____

Climb rating: ☆ ☆ ☆ ☆ ☆   Difficulty: 1 2 3 4 5

Companions: _____

_____

_____

Favourite moment: _____

_____

_____

Notes: _____

_____

_____

_____

_____

_____

_____

_____

_____

_____

_____

Meall nan Tarmachan
1,044m

Date: _____ Weather: _____ Temperature: _____

Start time: _____ End time: _____ Total distance: _____

Climb rating: ☆ ☆ ☆ ☆ ☆   Difficulty: 1 2 3 4 5

Companions: _____

_____

_____

Favourite moment: _____

_____

_____

Notes: _____

_____

_____

_____

_____

_____

_____

_____

_____

Stob Coir'an Albannaich
1,044m

Date: _____ Weather: _____ Temperature: _____

Start time: _____ End time: _____ Total distance: _____

Climb rating: ☆ ☆ ☆ ☆ ☆   Difficulty: 1 2 3 4 5

Companions: _____

_____

_____

Favourite moment: _____

_____

_____

Notes: _____

_____

_____

_____

_____

_____

_____

_____

_____

_____

Beinn Iutharn Mhor
1,045m

Date: _____ Weather: _____ Temperature: _____

Start time: _____ End time: _____ Total distance: _____

Climb rating: ☆ ☆ ☆ ☆ ☆   Difficulty: 1 2 3 4 5

Companions: _____

_____

_____

Favourite moment: _____

_____

_____

Notes: _____

_____

_____

_____

_____

_____

_____

_____

_____

Cruach Ardrain
1,046m

Date: _____ Weather: _____ Temperature: _____

Start time: _____ End time: _____ Total distance: _____

Climb rating: ☆ ☆ ☆ ☆ ☆   Difficulty: 1 2 3 4 5

Companions: _____

_____

_____

Favourite moment: _____

_____

_____

Notes: _____

_____

_____

_____

_____

_____

_____

_____

_____

Chno Dearg
1,046m

Date: _____ Weather: _____ Temperature: _____

Start time: _____ End time: _____ Total distance: _____

Climb rating: ☆ ☆ ☆ ☆ ☆   Difficulty: 1 2 3 4 5

Companions: _____

_____

_____

Favourite moment: _____

_____

_____

Notes: _____

_____

_____

_____

_____

_____

_____

_____

_____

_____

Ben Wyvis
1,046m

Date: _____ Weather: _____ Temperature: _____

Start time: _____ End time: _____ Total distance: _____

Climb rating: ☆ ☆ ☆ ☆ ☆   Difficulty: 1 2 3 4 5

Companions: _____

_____

_____

Favourite moment: _____

_____

_____

Notes: _____

_____

_____

_____

_____

_____

_____

_____

_____

_____

Creag Mhor (Lochay)
1,047m

Date: _____ Weather: _____ Temperature: _____

Start time: _____ End time: _____ Total distance: _____

Climb rating: ☆ ☆ ☆ ☆ ☆   Difficulty: 1 2 3 4 5

Companions: _____

_____

_____

Favourite moment: _____

_____

_____

Notes: _____

_____

_____

_____

_____

_____

_____

_____

Carn an t-Sagairt Mor
1,047m

Date: _____ Weather: _____ Temperature: _____

Start time: _____ End time: _____ Total distance: _____

Climb rating: ☆ ☆ ☆ ☆ ☆   Difficulty: 1 2 3 4 5

Companions: _____

_____

_____

Favourite moment: _____

_____

_____

Notes: _____

_____

_____

_____

_____

_____

_____

_____

_____

_____

Geal Charn (Laggan)
1,049m

Date: _____ Weather: _____ Temperature: _____

Start time: _____ End time: _____ Total distance: _____

Climb rating: ☆ ☆ ☆ ☆ ☆   Difficulty: 1 2 3 4 5

Companions: _____

_____

_____

Favourite moment: _____

_____

_____

Notes: _____

_____

_____

_____

_____

_____

_____

_____

_____

Sgurr Fhuar-thuill
1,049m

Date: _____ Weather: _____ Temperature: _____

Start time: _____ End time: _____ Total distance: _____

Climb rating: ☆ ☆ ☆ ☆ ☆   Difficulty: 1 2 3 4 5

Companions: _____

_____

_____

Favourite moment: _____

_____

_____

Notes: _____

_____

_____

_____

_____

_____

_____

_____

_____

_____

_____

Beinn a' Chaorainn
1,049m

Date: _____ Weather: _____ Temperature: _____

Start time: _____ End time: _____ Total distance: _____

Climb rating: ☆ ☆ ☆ ☆ ☆   Difficulty: 1 2 3 4 5

Companions: _____

_____

_____

Favourite moment: _____

_____

_____

Notes: _____

_____

_____

_____

_____

_____

_____

_____

_____

_____

Glas Tulaichean
1,051m

Date: _____ Weather: _____ Temperature: _____

Start time: _____ End time: _____ Total distance: _____

Climb rating: ☆ ☆ ☆ ☆ ☆   Difficulty: 1 2 3 4 5

Companions: _____

_____

_____

Favourite moment: _____

_____

_____

Notes: _____

_____

_____

_____

_____

_____

_____

_____

_____

_____

Sgurr a' Chaorachain
1,053m

Date: _____ Weather: _____ Temperature: _____

Start time: _____ End time: _____ Total distance: _____

Climb rating: ☆ ☆ ☆ ☆ ☆   Difficulty: 1 2 3 4 5

Companions: _____

_____

_____

Favourite moment: _____

_____

_____

Notes: _____

_____

_____

_____

_____

_____

_____

_____

_____

_____

Stob Poite Coire Ardair
1,054m

Date: _____ Weather: _____ Temperature: _____

Start time: _____ End time: _____ Total distance: _____

Climb rating: ☆ ☆ ☆ ☆ ☆ Difficulty: 1 2 3 4 5

Companions: _____

_____

_____

Favourite moment: _____

_____

_____

Notes: _____

_____

_____

_____

_____

_____

_____

_____

_____

_____

Toll Creagach
1,054m

Date: _____ Weather: _____ Temperature: _____

Start time: _____ End time: _____ Total distance: _____

Climb rating: ☆ ☆ ☆ ☆ ☆   Difficulty: 1 2 3 4 5

Companions: _____

_____

_____

Favourite moment: _____

_____

_____

Notes: _____

_____

_____

_____

_____

_____

_____

_____

_____

Na Gruagaichean
1,054m

Date: _____ Weather: _____ Temperature: _____

Start time: _____ End time: _____ Total distance: _____

Climb rating: ☆ ☆ ☆ ☆ ☆   Difficulty: 1 2 3 4 5

Companions: _____

_____

_____

Favourite moment: _____

_____

_____

Notes: _____

_____

_____

_____

_____

_____

_____

_____

_____

_____

_____

Liathach - Spidean a' Choire Leith
1,055m

Date: _____ Weather: _____ Temperature: _____

Start time: _____ End time: _____ Total distance: _____

Climb rating: ☆ ☆ ☆ ☆ ☆   Difficulty: 1 2 3 4 5

Companions: _____

_____

_____

Favourite moment: _____

_____

_____

Notes: _____

_____

_____

_____

_____

_____

_____

_____

_____

_____

An Teallach - Sgurr Fiona
1,059m

Date: _____ Weather: _____ Temperature: _____

Start time: _____ End time: _____ Total distance: _____

Climb rating: ☆ ☆ ☆ ☆ ☆   Difficulty: 1 2 3 4 5

Companions: _____

_____

_____

Favourite moment: _____

_____

_____

Notes: _____

_____

_____

_____

_____

_____

_____

_____

_____

An Teallach - Bidein a' Ghlas Thuill
1,063m

Date: _____ Weather: _____ Temperature: _____

Start time: _____ End time: _____ Total distance: _____

Climb rating: ☆ ☆ ☆ ☆ ☆   Difficulty: 1 2 3 4 5

Companions: _____

_____

_____

Favourite moment: _____

_____

_____

Notes: _____

_____

_____

_____

_____

_____

_____

_____

_____

_____

Cairn of Claise
1,064m

Date: _____ Weather: _____ Temperature: _____

Start time: _____ End time: _____ Total distance: _____

Climb rating: ☆ ☆ ☆ ☆ ☆   Difficulty: 1 2 3 4 5

Companions: _____

_____

_____

Favourite moment: _____

_____

_____

Notes: _____

_____

_____

_____

_____

_____

_____

_____

_____

_____

Glas Maol
1,068m

Date: _____   Weather: _____   Temperature: _____

Start time: _____   End time: _____   Total distance: _____

Climb rating: ☆ ☆ ☆ ☆ ☆   Difficulty: 1 2 3 4 5

Companions: _____

_____

_____

Favourite moment: _____

_____

_____

Notes: _____

_____

_____

_____

_____

_____

_____

_____

_____

_____

Sgurr Fhuaran
1,069m

Date: _____ Weather: _____ Temperature: _____

Start time: _____ End time: _____ Total distance: _____

Climb rating: ☆ ☆ ☆ ☆ ☆   Difficulty: 1 2 3 4 5

Companions: _____

_____

_____

Favourite moment: _____

_____

_____

Notes: _____

_____

_____

_____

_____

_____

_____

_____

_____

Meall Corranaich
1,069m

Date: _____ Weather: _____ Temperature: _____

Start time: _____ End time: _____ Total distance: _____

Climb rating: ☆ ☆ ☆ ☆ ☆   Difficulty: 1 2 3 4 5

Companions: _____

_____

_____

Favourite moment: _____

_____

_____

Notes: _____

_____

_____

_____

_____

_____

_____

_____

_____

_____

An Socach
1,069m

Date: _____ Weather: _____ Temperature: _____

Start time: _____ End time: _____ Total distance: _____

Climb rating: ☆ ☆ ☆ ☆ ☆   Difficulty: 1 2 3 4 5

Companions: _____

_____

_____

Favourite moment: _____

_____

_____

Notes: _____

_____

_____

_____

_____

_____

_____

_____

_____

_____

Beinn a' Ghlo - Braigh Coire Chruinn-bhagain
1,070m

Date: _____ Weather: _____ Temperature: _____

Start time: _____ End time: _____ Total distance: _____

Climb rating: ☆ ☆ ☆ ☆ ☆   Difficulty: 1 2 3 4 5

Companions: _____

_____

_____

Favourite moment: _____

_____

_____

Notes: _____

_____

_____

_____

_____

_____

_____

_____

_____

_____

Stob Coire Sgreamhach
1,072m

Date: _____ Weather: _____ Temperature: _____

Start time: _____ End time: _____ Total distance: _____

Climb rating: ☆ ☆ ☆ ☆ ☆   Difficulty: 1 2 3 4 5

Companions: _____

_____

_____

Favourite moment: _____

_____

_____

Notes: _____

_____

_____

_____

_____

_____

_____

_____

_____

_____

Beinn Dorain
1,076m

Date: _____ Weather: _____ Temperature: _____

Start time: _____ End time: _____ Total distance: _____

Climb rating: ☆ ☆ ☆ ☆ ☆   Difficulty: 1 2 3 4 5

Companions: _____

_____

_____

Favourite moment: _____

_____

_____

Notes: _____

_____

_____

_____

_____

_____

_____

_____

_____

Beinn Heasgarnich
1,077m

Date: _____ Weather: _____ Temperature: _____

Start time: _____ End time: _____ Total distance: _____

Climb rating: ☆ ☆ ☆ ☆ ☆   Difficulty: 1 2 3 4 5

Companions: _____

_____

_____

Favourite moment: _____

_____

_____

Notes: _____

_____

_____

_____

_____

_____

_____

_____

_____

_____

Ben Starav
1,080m

Date: _____ Weather: _____ Temperature: _____

Start time: _____ End time: _____ Total distance: _____

Climb rating: ☆ ☆ ☆ ☆ ☆   Difficulty: 1 2 3 4 5

Companions: _____

_____

_____

Favourite moment: _____

_____

_____

Notes: _____

_____

_____

_____

_____

_____

_____

_____

_____

Beinn a' Chreachain
1,081m

Date: _____ Weather: _____ Temperature: _____

Start time: _____ End time: _____ Total distance: _____

Climb rating: ☆ ☆ ☆ ☆ ☆   Difficulty: 1 2 3 4 5

Companions: _____

_____

_____

Favourite moment: _____

_____

_____

Notes: _____

_____

_____

_____

_____

_____

_____

_____

_____

_____

Schiehallion
1,083m

Date: _____ Weather: _____ Temperature: _____

Start time: _____ End time: _____ Total distance: _____

Climb rating: ☆ ☆ ☆ ☆ ☆   Difficulty: 1 2 3 4 5

Companions: _____

_____

_____

Favourite moment: _____

_____

_____

Notes: _____

_____

_____

_____

_____

_____

_____

_____

_____

Beinn a' Chaorainn (Avon)
1,083m

Date: _____ Weather: _____ Temperature: _____

Start time: _____ End time: _____ Total distance: _____

Climb rating: ☆ ☆ ☆ ☆ ☆   Difficulty: 1 2 3 4 5

Companions: _____

_____

_____

Favourite moment: _____

_____

_____

Notes: _____

_____

_____

_____

_____

_____

_____

_____

_____

Sgurr a' Choire Ghlas
1,083m

Date: _____ Weather: _____ Temperature: _____

Start time: _____ End time: _____ Total distance: _____

Climb rating: ☆ ☆ ☆ ☆ ☆   Difficulty: 1 2 3 4 5

Companions: _____

_____

_____

Favourite moment: _____

_____

_____

Notes: _____

_____

_____

_____

_____

_____

_____

_____

_____

Beinn Dearg (Inverlael)
1,084m

Date: _____ Weather: _____ Temperature: _____

Start time: _____ End time: _____ Total distance: _____

Climb rating: ☆ ☆ ☆ ☆ ☆   Difficulty: 1 2 3 4 5

Companions: _____

_____

_____

Favourite moment: _____

_____

_____

Notes: _____

_____

_____

_____

_____

_____

_____

_____

_____

_____

Beinn a' Chlachair
1,087m

Date: _____ Weather: _____ Temperature: _____

Start time: _____ End time: _____ Total distance: _____

Climb rating: ☆ ☆ ☆ ☆ ☆   Difficulty: 1 2 3 4 5

Companions: _____

_____

_____

Favourite moment: _____

_____

_____

Notes: _____

_____

_____

_____

_____

_____

_____

_____

_____

Stob Ghabhar
1,090m

Date: _____ Weather: _____ Temperature: _____

Start time: _____ End time: _____ Total distance: _____

Climb rating: ☆ ☆ ☆ ☆ ☆   Difficulty: 1 2 3 4 5

Companions: _____

_____

_____

Favourite moment: _____

_____

_____

Notes: _____

_____

_____

_____

_____

_____

_____

_____

_____

_____

Bynack More
1,090m

Date: _____ Weather: _____ Temperature: _____

Start time: _____ End time: _____ Total distance: _____

Climb rating: ☆ ☆ ☆ ☆ ☆   Difficulty: 1 2 3 4 5

Companions: _____

_____

_____

Favourite moment: _____

_____

_____

Notes: _____

_____

_____

_____

_____

_____

_____

_____

_____

_____

Sgurr nan Clach Geala
1,093m

Date: _____ Weather: _____ Temperature: _____

Start time: _____ End time: _____ Total distance: _____

Climb rating: ☆ ☆ ☆ ☆ ☆   Difficulty: 1 2 3 4 5

Companions: _____

_____

_____

Favourite moment: _____

_____

_____

Notes: _____

_____

_____

_____

_____

_____

_____

_____

_____

_____

_____

Sgurr Choinnich Mor
1,094m

Date: _____ Weather: _____ Temperature: _____

Start time: _____ End time: _____ Total distance: _____

Climb rating: ☆ ☆ ☆ ☆ ☆   Difficulty: 1 2 3 4 5

Companions: _____

_____

_____

Favourite moment: _____

_____

_____

Notes: _____

_____

_____

_____

_____

_____

_____

_____

_____

Sgurr a 'Mhaim
1,099m

Date: _____ Weather: _____ Temperature: _____

Start time: _____ End time: _____ Total distance: _____

Climb rating: ☆ ☆ ☆ ☆ ☆   Difficulty: 1 2 3 4 5

Companions: _____

_____

_____

Favourite moment: _____

_____

_____

Notes: _____

_____

_____

_____

_____

_____

_____

_____

_____

_____

Creise
1,100m

Date: _____ Weather: _____ Temperature: _____

Start time: _____ End time: _____ Total distance: _____

Climb rating: ☆ ☆ ☆ ☆ ☆   Difficulty: 1 2 3 4 5

Companions: _____

_____

_____

Favourite moment: _____

_____

_____

Notes: _____

_____

_____

_____

_____

_____

_____

_____

_____

_____

Mullach Fraoch-choire
1,102m

Date: _____ Weather: _____ Temperature: _____

Start time: _____ End time: _____ Total distance: _____

Climb rating: ☆ ☆ ☆ ☆ ☆   Difficulty: 1 2 3 4 5

Companions: _____

_____

_____

Favourite moment: _____

_____

_____

Notes: _____

_____

_____

_____

_____

_____

_____

_____

_____

_____

_____

Beinn Ghlas
1,103m

Date: _____ Weather: _____ Temperature: _____

Start time: _____ End time: _____ Total distance: _____

Climb rating: ☆ ☆ ☆ ☆ ☆   Difficulty: 1 2 3 4 5

Companions: _____

_____

_____

Favourite moment: _____

_____

_____

Notes: _____

_____

_____

_____

_____

_____

_____

_____

_____

_____

Beinn Eibhinn
1,103m

Date: _____ Weather: _____ Temperature: _____

Start time: _____ End time: _____ Total distance: _____

Climb rating: ☆ ☆ ☆ ☆ ☆   Difficulty: 1 2 3 4 5

Companions: _____

_____

_____

Favourite moment: _____

_____

_____

Notes: _____

_____

_____

_____

_____

_____

_____

_____

_____

_____

Stob a' Choire Mheadhoin
1,105m

Date: _____ Weather: _____ Temperature: _____

Start time: _____ End time: _____ Total distance: _____

Climb rating: ☆ ☆ ☆ ☆ ☆   Difficulty: 1 2 3 4 5

Companions: _____

_____

_____

Favourite moment: _____

_____

_____

Notes: _____

_____

_____

_____

_____

_____

_____

_____

_____

_____

Meall a' Bhuiridh
1,108m

Date: _____ Weather: _____ Temperature: _____

Start time: _____ End time: _____ Total distance: _____

Climb rating: ☆ ☆ ☆ ☆ ☆   Difficulty: 1 2 3 4 5

Companions: _____

_____

_____

Favourite moment: _____

_____

_____

Notes: _____

_____

_____

_____

_____

_____

_____

_____

_____

_____

Sgurr Mor (Franaichs)
1,109m

Date: _____ Weather: _____ Temperature: _____

Start time: _____ End time: _____ Total distance: _____

Climb rating: ☆ ☆ ☆ ☆ ☆   Difficulty: 1 2 3 4 5

Companions: _____

_____

_____

Favourite moment: _____

_____

_____

Notes: _____

_____

_____

_____

_____

_____

_____

_____

_____

Sgurr nan Conbhairean
1,109m

Date: _____ Weather: _____ Temperature: _____

Start time: _____ End time: _____ Total distance: _____

Climb rating: ☆ ☆ ☆ ☆ ☆   Difficulty: 1 2 3 4 5

Companions: _____

_____

_____

Favourite moment: _____

_____

_____

Notes: _____

_____

_____

_____

_____

_____

_____

_____

_____

_____

Carn a' Choire Bhoidheach
1,110m

Date: _____ Weather: _____ Temperature: _____

Start time: _____ End time: _____ Total distance: _____

Climb rating: ☆ ☆ ☆ ☆ ☆   Difficulty: 1 2 3 4 5

Companions: _____

_____

_____

Favourite moment: _____

_____

_____

Notes: _____

_____

_____

_____

_____

_____

_____

_____

_____

_____

Tom a' Choinich
1,112m

Date: _____ Weather: _____ Temperature: _____

Start time: _____ End time: _____ Total distance: _____

Climb rating: ☆ ☆ ☆ ☆ ☆   Difficulty: 1 2 3 4 5

Companions: _____

_____

_____

Favourite moment: _____

_____

_____

Notes: _____

_____

_____

_____

_____

_____

_____

_____

_____

_____

Monadh Mor
1,113m

Date: _____ Weather: _____ Temperature: _____

Start time: _____ End time: _____ Total distance: _____

Climb rating: ☆ ☆ ☆ ☆ ☆   Difficulty: 1 2 3 4 5

Companions: _____

_____

_____

Favourite moment: _____

_____

_____

Notes: _____

_____

_____

_____

_____

_____

_____

_____

_____

_____

Stob Coire Easain
1,115m

Date: _____ Weather: _____ Temperature: _____

Start time: _____ End time: _____ Total distance: _____

Climb rating: ☆ ☆ ☆ ☆ ☆   Difficulty: 1 2 3 4 5

Companions: _____

_____

_____

Favourite moment: _____

_____

_____

Notes: _____

_____

_____

_____

_____

_____

_____

_____

_____

_____

_____

Aonach Beag (Alder)
1,116m

Date: _____ Weather: _____ Temperature: _____

Start time: _____ End time: _____ Total distance: _____

Climb rating: ☆ ☆ ☆ ☆ ☆   Difficulty: 1 2 3 4 5

Companions: _____

_____

_____

Favourite moment: _____

_____

_____

Notes: _____

_____

_____

_____

_____

_____

_____

_____

_____

_____

Stob Coire an Laoigh
1,116m

Date: _____ Weather: _____ Temperature: _____

Start time: _____ End time: _____ Total distance: _____

Climb rating: ☆ ☆ ☆ ☆ ☆   Difficulty: 1 2 3 4 5

Companions: _____

_____

_____

Favourite moment: _____

_____

_____

Notes: _____

_____

_____

_____

_____

_____

_____

_____

_____

_____

_____

An Stuc
1,117m

Date: _____ Weather: _____ Temperature: _____

Start time: _____ End time: _____ Total distance: _____

Climb rating: ☆ ☆ ☆ ☆ ☆   Difficulty: 1 2 3 4 5

Companions: _____

_____

_____

Favourite moment: _____

_____

_____

Notes: _____

_____

_____

_____

_____

_____

_____

_____

_____

Sgor Gaoith
1,118m

Date: _____ Weather: _____ Temperature: _____

Start time: _____ End time: _____ Total distance: _____

Climb rating: ☆ ☆ ☆ ☆ ☆   Difficulty: 1 2 3 4 5

Companions: _____

_____

_____

Favourite moment: _____

_____

_____

Notes: _____

_____

_____

_____

_____

_____

_____

_____

_____

_____

A' Chralaig
1,120m

Date: _____ Weather: _____ Temperature: _____

Start time: _____ End time: _____ Total distance: _____

Climb rating: ☆ ☆ ☆ ☆ ☆   Difficulty: 1 2 3 4 5

Companions: _____

_____

_____

Favourite moment: _____

_____

_____

Notes: _____

_____

_____

_____

_____

_____

_____

_____

_____

_____

Beinn a' Ghlo - Carn nan Gabhar
1,122m

Date: _____ Weather: _____ Temperature: _____

Start time: _____ End time: _____ Total distance: _____

Climb rating: ☆ ☆ ☆ ☆ ☆   Difficulty: 1 2 3 4 5

Companions: _____

_____

_____

Favourite moment: _____

_____

_____

Notes: _____

_____

_____

_____

_____

_____

_____

_____

_____

_____

Meall Garbh (Lawers)
1,123m

Date: _____ Weather: _____ Temperature: _____

Start time: _____ End time: _____ Total distance: _____

Climb rating: ☆ ☆ ☆ ☆ ☆   Difficulty: 1 2 3 4 5

Companions: _____

_____

_____

Favourite moment: _____

_____

_____

Notes: _____

_____

_____

_____

_____

_____

_____

_____

_____

Ben Cruachan
1,127m

Date: _____ Weather: _____ Temperature: _____

Start time: _____ End time: _____ Total distance: _____

Climb rating: ☆ ☆ ☆ ☆ ☆   Difficulty: 1 2 3 4 5

Companions: _____

_____

_____

Favourite moment: _____

_____

_____

Notes: _____

_____

_____

_____

_____

_____

_____

_____

_____

_____

_____

Creag Meagaidh
1,128m

Date: _____ Weather: _____ Temperature: _____

Start time: _____ End time: _____ Total distance: _____

Climb rating: ☆ ☆ ☆ ☆ ☆   Difficulty: 1 2 3 4 5

Companions: _____

_____

_____

Favourite moment: _____

_____

_____

Notes: _____

_____

_____

_____

_____

_____

_____

_____

_____

_____

_____

An Riabhachan
1,129m

Date: _____ Weather: _____ Temperature: _____

Start time: _____ End time: _____ Total distance: _____

Climb rating: ☆ ☆ ☆ ☆ ☆   Difficulty: 1 2 3 4 5

Companions: _____

_____

_____

Favourite moment: _____

_____

_____

Notes: _____

_____

_____

_____

_____

_____

_____

_____

_____

_____

Ben Lui
1,130m

Date: _____ Weather: _____ Temperature: _____

Start time: _____ End time: _____ Total distance: _____

Climb rating: ☆ ☆ ☆ ☆ ☆   Difficulty: 1 2 3 4 5

Companions: _____

_____

_____

Favourite moment: _____

_____

_____

Notes: _____

_____

_____

_____

_____

_____

_____

_____

_____

Binnein Mor
1,130m

Date: _____ Weather: _____ Temperature: _____

Start time: _____ End time: _____ Total distance: _____

Climb rating: ☆ ☆ ☆ ☆ ☆   Difficulty: 1 2 3 4 5

Companions: _____

_____

_____

Favourite moment: _____

_____

_____

Notes: _____

_____

_____

_____

_____

_____

_____

_____

_____

_____

Geal-Charm (Alder)
1,132m

Date: _____ Weather: _____ Temperature: _____

Start time: _____ End time: _____ Total distance: _____

Climb rating: ☆ ☆ ☆ ☆ ☆   Difficulty: 1 2 3 4 5

Companions: _____

_____

_____

Favourite moment: _____

_____

_____

Notes: _____

_____

_____

_____

_____

_____

_____

_____

_____

_____

Ben Alder
1,148m

Date: _____ Weather: _____ Temperature: _____

Start time: _____ End time: _____ Total distance: _____

Climb rating: ☆ ☆ ☆ ☆ ☆   Difficulty: 1 2 3 4 5

Companions: _____

_____

_____

Favourite moment: _____

_____

_____

Notes: _____

_____

_____

_____

_____

_____

_____

_____

_____

_____

Bidean nam Bian
1,149m

Date: _____ Weather: _____ Temperature: _____

Start time: _____ End time: _____ Total distance: _____

Climb rating: ☆ ☆ ☆ ☆ ☆   Difficulty: 1 2 3 4 5

Companions: _____

_____

_____

Favourite moment: _____

_____

_____

Notes: _____

_____

_____

_____

_____

_____

_____

_____

_____

_____

Sgurr nan Ceathreamhnan
1,151m

Date: _____ Weather: _____ Temperature: _____

Start time: _____ End time: _____ Total distance: _____

Climb rating: ☆ ☆ ☆ ☆ ☆   Difficulty: 1 2 3 4 5

Companions: _____

_____

_____

Favourite moment: _____

_____

_____

Notes: _____

_____

_____

_____

_____

_____

_____

_____

_____

_____

Sgurr na Lapaich
1,151m

Date: _____ Weather: _____ Temperature: _____

Start time: _____ End time: _____ Total distance: _____

Climb rating: ☆ ☆ ☆ ☆ ☆   Difficulty: 1 2 3 4 5

Companions: _____

_____

_____

Favourite moment: _____

_____

_____

Notes: _____

_____

_____

_____

_____

_____

_____

_____

_____

_____

Derry Cairngorm
1,155m

Date: _____   Weather: _____   Temperature: _____

Start time: _____   End time: _____   Total distance: _____

Climb rating: ☆ ☆ ☆ ☆ ☆   Difficulty: 1 2 3 4 5

Companions: _____

_____

_____

Favourite moment: _____

_____

_____

Notes: _____

_____

_____

_____

_____

_____

_____

_____

_____

_____

Lochnagar (Cac Carn Beag)
1,156m

Date: _____ Weather: _____ Temperature: _____

Start time: _____ End time: _____ Total distance: _____

Climb rating: ☆ ☆ ☆ ☆ ☆   Difficulty: 1 2 3 4 5

Companions: _____

_____

_____

Favourite moment: _____

_____

_____

Notes: _____

_____

_____

_____

_____

_____

_____

_____

_____

Beinn Bhrotain
1,157m

Date: _____ Weather: _____ Temperature: _____

Start time: _____ End time: _____ Total distance: _____

Climb rating: ☆ ☆ ☆ ☆ ☆   Difficulty: 1 2 3 4 5

Companions: _____

_____

_____

Favourite moment: _____

_____

_____

Notes: _____

_____

_____

_____

_____

_____

_____

_____

_____

_____

Stob Binnein
1,165m

Date: _____ Weather: _____ Temperature: _____

Start time: _____ End time: _____ Total distance: _____

Climb rating: ☆ ☆ ☆ ☆ ☆   Difficulty: 1 2 3 4 5

Companions: _____

_____

_____

Favourite moment: _____

_____

_____

Notes: _____

_____

_____

_____

_____

_____

_____

_____

_____

_____

Ben Avon
1,171m

Date: _____   Weather: _____   Temperature: _____

Start time: _____   End time: _____   Total distance: _____

Climb rating: ☆ ☆ ☆ ☆ ☆   Difficulty: 1 2 3 4 5

Companions: _____

_____

_____

Favourite moment: _____

_____

_____

Notes: _____

_____

_____

_____

_____

_____

_____

_____

_____

_____

Ben More (Crianlarich)
1,174m

Date: _____ Weather: _____ Temperature: _____

Start time: _____ End time: _____ Total distance: _____

Climb rating: ☆ ☆ ☆ ☆ ☆   Difficulty: 1 2 3 4 5

Companions: _____

_____

_____

Favourite moment: _____

_____

_____

Notes: _____

_____

_____

_____

_____

_____

_____

_____

_____

_____

Stob Choire Claurigh
1,177m

Date: _____ Weather: _____ Temperature: _____

Start time: _____ End time: _____ Total distance: _____

Climb rating: ☆ ☆ ☆ ☆ ☆   Difficulty: 1 2 3 4 5

Companions: _____

_____

_____

Favourite moment: _____

_____

_____

Notes: _____

_____

_____

_____

_____

_____

_____

_____

_____

_____

Mam Sodhail
1,179m

Date: _____ Weather: _____ Temperature: _____

Start time: _____ End time: _____ Total distance: _____

Climb rating: ☆ ☆ ☆ ☆ ☆   Difficulty: 1 2 3 4 5

Companions: _____

_____

_____

Favourite moment: _____

_____

_____

Notes: _____

_____

_____

_____

_____

_____

_____

_____

_____

_____

Carn Eighe
1,183m

Date: _____ Weather: _____ Temperature: _____

Start time: _____ End time: _____ Total distance: _____

Climb rating: ☆ ☆ ☆ ☆ ☆   Difficulty: 1 2 3 4 5

Companions: _____

_____

_____

Favourite moment: _____

_____

_____

Notes: _____

_____

_____

_____

_____

_____

_____

_____

_____

_____

Beinn Mheadhoin
1,183m

Date: _____ Weather: _____ Temperature: _____

Start time: _____ End time: _____ Total distance: _____

Climb rating: ☆ ☆ ☆ ☆ ☆   Difficulty: 1 2 3 4 5

Companions: _____

_____

_____

Favourite moment: _____

_____

_____

Notes: _____

_____

_____

_____

_____

_____

_____

_____

_____

_____

Beinn a' Bhuird
1,197m

Date: _____ Weather: _____ Temperature: _____

Start time: _____ End time: _____ Total distance: _____

Climb rating: ☆ ☆ ☆ ☆ ☆   Difficulty: 1 2 3 4 5

Companions: _____

_____

_____

Favourite moment: _____

_____

_____

Notes: _____

_____

_____

_____

_____

_____

_____

_____

_____

_____

_____

Ben Lawers
1,214m

Date: _____ Weather: _____ Temperature: _____

Start time: _____ End time: _____ Total distance: _____

Climb rating: ☆ ☆ ☆ ☆ ☆   Difficulty: 1 2 3 4 5

Companions: _____

_____

_____

Favourite moment: _____

_____

_____

Notes: _____

_____

_____

_____

_____

_____

_____

_____

_____

_____

Carn Mor Dearg
1,220m

Date: _____ Weather: _____ Temperature: _____

Start time: _____ End time: _____ Total distance: _____

Climb rating: ☆ ☆ ☆ ☆ ☆ Difficulty: 1 2 3 4 5

Companions: _____

_____

_____

Favourite moment: _____

_____

_____

Notes: _____

_____

_____

_____

_____

_____

_____

_____

_____

_____

_____

Aonach Mor
1,220m

Date: _____ Weather: _____ Temperature: _____

Start time: _____ End time: _____ Total distance: _____

Climb rating: ☆ ☆ ☆ ☆ ☆   Difficulty: 1 2 3 4 5

Companions: _____

_____

_____

Favourite moment: _____

_____

_____

Notes: _____

_____

_____

_____

_____

_____

_____

_____

_____

_____

Aonach Beag (Nevis)
1,234m

Date: _____ Weather: _____ Temperature: _____

Start time: _____ End time: _____ Total distance: _____

Climb rating: ☆ ☆ ☆ ☆ ☆   Difficulty: 1 2 3 4 5

Companions: _____

_____

_____

Favourite moment: _____

_____

_____

Notes: _____

_____

_____

_____

_____

_____

_____

_____

_____

Cairn Gorm
1,245m

Date: _____ Weather: _____ Temperature: _____

Start time: _____ End time: _____ Total distance: _____

Climb rating: ☆ ☆ ☆ ☆ ☆   Difficulty: 1 2 3 4 5

Companions: _____

_____

_____

Favourite moment: _____

_____

_____

Notes: _____

_____

_____

_____

_____

_____

_____

_____

_____

Sgor an Lochain Uaine
1,258m

Date: _____ Weather: _____ Temperature: _____

Start time: _____ End time: _____ Total distance: _____

Climb rating: ☆ ☆ ☆ ☆ ☆   Difficulty: 1 2 3 4 5

Companions: _____

_____

_____

Favourite moment: _____

_____

_____

Notes: _____

_____

_____

_____

_____

_____

_____

_____

_____

Cairn Toul
1,291m

Date: _____ Weather: _____ Temperature: _____

Start time: _____ End time: _____ Total distance: _____

Climb rating: ☆ ☆ ☆ ☆ ☆. Difficulty: 1 2 3 4 5

Companions: _____

_____

_____

Favourite moment: _____

_____

_____

Notes: _____

_____

_____

_____

_____

_____

_____

_____

_____

Braeriach
1,296m

Date: _____ Weather: _____ Temperature: _____

Start time: _____ End time: _____ Total distance: _____

Climb rating: ☆ ☆ ☆ ☆ ☆   Difficulty: 1 2 3 4 5

Companions: _____

_____

_____

Favourite moment: _____

_____

_____

Notes: _____

_____

_____

_____

_____

_____

_____

_____

_____

_____

Ben Macdui
1,309m

Date: _____ Weather: _____ Temperature: _____

Start time: _____ End time: _____ Total distance: _____

Climb rating: ☆ ☆ ☆ ☆ ☆   Difficulty: 1 2 3 4 5

Companions: _____

_____

_____

Favourite moment: _____

_____

_____

Notes: _____

_____

_____

_____

_____

_____

_____

_____

_____

_____

Ben Nevis
1,345m

Date: _____ Weather: _____ Temperature: _____

Start time: _____ End time: _____ Total distance: _____

Climb rating: ☆ ☆ ☆ ☆ ☆   Difficulty: 1 2 3 4 5

Companions: _____

_____

_____

Favourite moment: _____

_____

_____

Notes: _____

_____

_____

_____

_____

_____

_____

_____

_____

_____

Printed in Great Britain
by Amazon